DISCARD
ESCH LIBRARY
LAKELAND UNIVERSITY

D0225281

Conscientious Sorcerers

813.54 F793c
Fox, Robert Elliot, 1944-
Conscientious sorcerers

CONSCIENTIOUS SORCERERS

The Black Postmodernist Fiction of LeRoi Jones/Amiri Baraka, Ishmael Reed, and Samuel R. Delany

ROBERT ELLIOT FOX

CONTRIBUTIONS IN AFRO-AMERICAN AND
AFRICAN STUDIES, NUMBER 106

GREENWOOD PRESS

Library
Lakeland College

NEW YORK
WESTPORT, CONNECTICUT
LONDON

Library of Congress Cataloging-in-Publication Data

Fox, Robert Elliot, 1944–
 Conscientious sorcerers.

 (Contributions in Afro-American and African
studies, ISSN 0069-9624 ; no. 106)
 Bibliography: p.
 Includes index.
 1. American fiction—20th century—History and
criticism. 2. American fiction—Afro-American
authors—History and criticism. 3. Baraka, Imamu
Amiri, 1934–   —Criticism and interpretation.
4. Reed, Ishmael, 1938–   —Criticism and interpretation. 5. Delany, Samuel R., 1942–   —Criticism and
interpretation. I. Title. II. Series.
 PS153.N5F69 1987 813'.54'09896 86-25754
 ISBN 0-313-25033-2 (lib. bdg. : alk. paper)

Copyright © 1987 by Robert Elliot Fox

All rights reserved. No portion of this book may be
reproduced, by any process or technique, without the
express written consent of the publisher.

Library of Congress Catalog Card Number: 86-25754
ISBN: 0-313-25033-2
ISSN: 0069-9624

First published in 1987

Greenwood Press, Inc.
88 Post Road West, Westport, Connecticut 06881

Printed in the United States of America

The paper used in this book complies with the
Permanent Paper Standard issued by the National
Information Standards Organization (Z39.48-1984).

10 9 8 7 6 5 4 3 2 1

For my father
and in memory
of my mother

Contents

viii   *Contents*

Preface

Amiri Baraka (LeRoi Jones), Ishmael Reed, and Samuel R. Delany are three of the most important and gifted American authors to have emerged in the tumultuous period of the 1960s, when the complacencies of the previous decade were disordered significantly. The three are black, and it is within the context of Afro-American literature that they will be examined here. Their blackness, however, is not a limiting factor—the "exotic" label it would have been in an earlier setting—but rather an opening of the aperture of our heretofore narrowly focused cultural vision, enabling "discoveries" of what was always present but studiedly masked or unacknowledged. One of the recognitions that follows from this is just how really American are these and other ethnically categorized writers. Afro-American literature had its idiom—a black idiom—but then had to find its own trajectory, which is broadly American if one conceives of America (as one finally must) as much more than the achievements and experiences of a single cultural entity.

Of the three authors under scrutiny, Baraka has had the greatest impact and influence on the black American sociopolitical/creative struggle, Delany the least, although in my estimation Delany's vision is ultimately more radical than Baraka's, which functions within a rather conventional framework. Delany is the most profoundly imaginative and intellectual of the three, Reed the most experimental and colloquial. Delany is the most meditative, the most self-conscious craftsman; Reed is the most spontaneous, the most brazen; Baraka is the most chameleon-like, the most demagogic, the most centered in hardcore politics, though politics infuses the works of Reed and Delany as well.

Baraka and Reed are engaged in the practice of ethnopoetics, while Delany's enterprise has the apparent "colorlessness" of technique per se; that is, while race is a factor in the worlds of Delany's fiction, it is not a foregrounded concern in the same way that it is in the works of the other two authors under examination.

Despite the "experimental" style, Baraka's—actually LeRoi Jones's—fiction is experientially very much within the confessional/ autobiographical mode which constitutes a significant part of the canon of Afro-American literature. Reed's works are, on one level, a deconstruction of that black literary tradition and, simultaneously, a reassertion of the folk aesthetic that has always shaped (directly or indirectly) the form and content of black writing and black art. Delany, however, appropriated new territory for black writing by directing his imaginative energies into a future orientation that opened up realms of pure possibility. This allowed a disengagement of Delany's works from the weighty determinants of actual history that constitute an inevitable burden (both as a problematic and as a responsibility) for black writers.

In the past decade, while Baraka has produced very little fiction, Reed has published three novels, which I have included in this study. Considering the size of his oeuvre, in the case of Delany I have been constrained by my given limits to focus on those works that have appeared since my initial investigation, which, indeed, are more aptly termed postmodernist than the writings of his early period.

I wish to acknowledge my deep indebtedness to Henry Louis Gates, Jr., and Joe Weixlmann for their very kind and enthusiastic support, for which I am extremely grateful.

For their encouragement, inspiration, and affectionate proddings when I needed them most, I also wish to thank Jerzy and Anna Wypych, Barry and Janice Ward, Andrew Gordon, Stan Sanvel Rubin, and Jennifer Washington, as well as my friends and former colleagues at the University of Ife in Nigeria, from whom I learned so much.

I also want to express my loving appreciation to Irene Belcher, who helped nurture me and to whom, in a very real sense, the roots of this enterprise can be traced.

Finally, 'Toyin Dare: when I needed you there, there you were. *Modupe-o.*

Conscientious
Sorcerers

1

Introduction

Desire, writing, do not remain in place, but pass one over the other.

Blanchot, *The Writing of the Disaster*

The radical inversion of Western systems of belief and order that LeRoi Jones/Amiri Baraka,[1] Ishmael Reed, and Samuel R. Delany engage in can be termed "mythoclasm," the drastic demystification of ideological signs that have been turned into false universals (Foster, 5). Their praxis as artists involves countering the hegemonic code inscribed by the master culture with alternatives of discourse and desire (transformational longings).

Borrowing the concept of the triangularity of desire from Rene Girard, I have proposed three formulations which are relevant to the black experience. The first is historical and relates to slavery as a vital component of the so-called triangular trade, the dynamic of early imperialist economy. That is, actually, the Triangle of European Desire (fig. 1). Europe is at the apex; the colonies (Africa, the Americas) are at the base. Raw materials shipped from the New World to Europe were turned into manufactured goods that were shipped to Africa to be exchanged for slaves (black gold), who were then transported to the Americas ("raw materials" changed into "things," the process that Césaire has termed "chosification").

This triangle forms the basis for black dispossession, encompassing the infamous Middle Passage which resulted in the Diaspora. It creates an Afro-American legacy characterized by the

Figure 1
The Triangle of European Desire

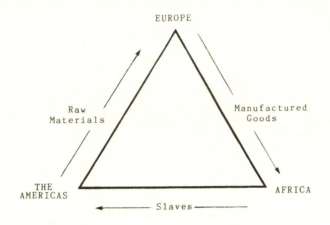

double consciousness W. E. B. DuBois articulated in *The Souls of Black Folk*; yet it is a legacy with its own special continuity, a singular soulness that provides the binding energy of a culture. This energy took on its particular form during slavery; to use an expression that Reed has imagineered so effectively, it "jes grew," the product of genius that thrives in adversity. Long after slavery ended, former slaves provided living testimony to the solidness of tradition; they appear in the literature in the person of such diverse characters as Aunt Hager Williams in Langston Hughes's *Not Without Laughter* and the ever-present spirit of the grandfather in Ralph Ellison's *Invisible Man*. They are the *velhos pretos*, the old black slaves invoked ancestrally in Brazilian Candomblé worship as a reminder of origins. It is this continuity that enables Ntozake Shange to refer to "the slaves who were ourselves" in her novel *Sassafrass, Cypress, and Indigo* (28). The seeming attempts to create discontinuities in the tradition may provide the reason for the apparent put-down of the New Negro in Reed's novel *Mumbo Jumbo*. What is really "new" about the New Negro? Is it the degree of assimilation into white culture, a transition from "nigger" to "niggerati"? For Reed, the folk roots of black culture are the creative province of the "old" Negro, who personifies changing sameness.

As inheritors of this tradition, the three authors deal with the problems and the limits of freedom and with forms of enslavement.

Jones/Baraka	Reed	Delany
Enslavement to white values and the capitalist economic system	Literal slavery Enslavement to "universals"	Literal slavery Sexual slavery Semiotic slavery

Literal emancipation does not end the legacy of slavery or preclude the fact of neo-slavery, as the American experience demonstrates. South Africa, where slavery was abolished even earlier (1834), is a still more poignant example. Moreover, if there is truth in the Freudian idea that our disturbances derive not only from oppression but also from desire ("Slavery is the future of mastery"; "Enslavement is always the final result of desire" [Girard, 170, 180]), then the recognition that ending one form of slavery does not necessarily ensure freedom becomes more valid. Baraka and Reed, who have consciously placed themselves in the tradition of those slaves who earned the reputation of "troublesome property," nevertheless confront the equally troublesome reality of European hegemonic codes that must be transcended if one's authenticity is to be unshackled. The narrator in *The System of Dante's Hell* pours a verbal caustic over the white-oriented consciousness of his earlier self, an exorcism that precedes LeRoi Jones's transformation into Amiri Baraka and his embrace of nationalism and, subsequently, of communism. In *The Freelance Pallbearers*, Reed's Bukka Doopeyduk is mesmerized by the zombifying creeds of the scatological circus of HARRY SAM; in *Mumbo Jumbo*, Woodrow Wilson Jefferson, a black pragmatist from Rē-mōte, Mississippi, leaves the farm and heads north where he lands a job as a Negro Viewpoint, while in actuality he is being programmed into a Talking Android; in *Flight to Canada*, Raven Quickskill and his fellow fugitive slaves seek a promised land of freedom that proves to be an ever-receding horizon. Delany's characters frequently embark upon quests that always seem to lead back to the wasteland, or else they leap from restraint into possibility only to be confronted with new agonies of choice and the limits imposed by their own (pre)dispositions. (In fact, as we shall see, one of the problematics in Delany's work

Figure 2
The Triangle of Black Desire: Pan-African Unity

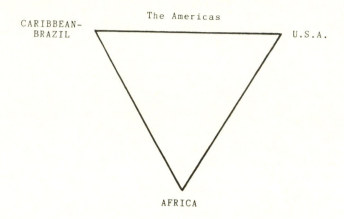

is that the desire to eradicate slavery is intimately bound with the slavery of desire.)

The next triangle is one of black desire and pertains to the dream of pan-African unity (fig. 2). The three points here are Africa, the Caribbean/Brazil, and the United States. Africa and the Caribbean/Brazil could provide the base since they are still "underdeveloped," but I have turned the triangle upside down to position Africa at "the root." Perhaps the lines forming the three sides of the triangle should be dotted as a reminder that although they demonstrate absolute links, pan-African unity, even on the African continent itself, remains a dream. This is the triangle of the longing for repossession.

The third triangle is also one of black desire (fig. 3). It deals with rhythm and recurrence, reclamation and redemption. It is a triangle inscribed in a circle, to engage the three points demarcating past, present, and future in a context of nonlinearity, of continuity. "What goes around, comes around." Here I have, at the risk of appearing to overschematize, placed Baraka, Reed, and Delany at separate points: Baraka, the present; Reed, the past; Delany, the future. Going counterclockwise around the circle, the present returns to the past, and the past leads to the future—because the past

Figure 3
The Triangle of Black Desire: Past, Present, and Future

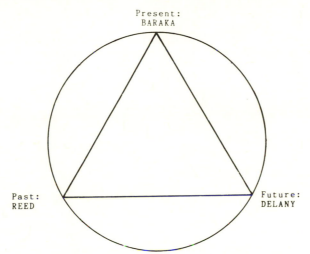

Present:
BARAKA

Past:
REED

Future:
DELANY

is prologue and the present is always in transition. Reed looks back in order to go forward with greater completeness, for the way in which we (re)conceive the past determines the kind of future we are predicating. Delany's fantasy trilogy also evokes the past and links it to the present, which he critiques with his future fictions; hence, the circle can be read clockwise as well.[2]

Baraka's trajectory, which propelled him through black nationalism to communism, has, with the exception of his Beat period apolitical aestheticism, generally given priority to politics (fig. 4). Although the revolutionary determinism of the Black Arts movement did not have the kind of detrimental effect on Baraka's work that it had on more naive or less gifted artists—thus enabling Baraka, along with a number of other committed creative individuals, to open a henceforth undeniable space for blackness in the whitewashed cultural castle—the danger of ideological closure with its strangulating effect on art's fullest energies has been increasingly evident over the last decade. When I suggest that this perhaps overdriven thrust into a stultifying arena for literary achievement has happened via what I term the psychopolitical (fig. 5), I am referring to the complex dynamics of person and praxis that are everywhere revealed in the fiction, which is one reason I believe close readings

Figure 4
Essential Priorities of Baraka, Reed, and Delany

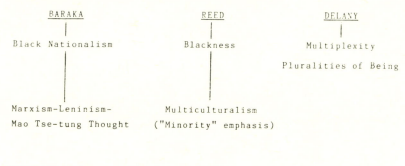

of *The System of Dante's Hell* and *Tales* care crucial for a broader understanding of Jones/Baraka's canon and career. These autobiographical fictions are more revealing of the inner life, the psychodynamics of being, than is *The Autobiography of LeRoi Jones/Amiri Baraka*, which indeed sometimes fictionalizes, though it lacks the power of language manifested in *System* and *Tales*, and which also seems to be largely an exercise in political self-justification.

Reed began with a primary emphasis on blackness, as another participant in the enterprise of establishing Afro-America's own unique identity and the degree of its penetration into the history and mentality of America as a whole. However, his recognition of the fact that the American pie has been baked from a variety of recipes and ingredients led Reed into a perspective that could aptly be termed multicultural with a "minority" emphasis (fig. 4). All along, his priority has been to culture(s), but in moving beyond the boundaries of an Afrocentric vision to one that is American in a pluralistic sense, Reed helped to open a space for blackness to reinterpret itself, to finally see itself as one great heterogene in an even vaster heterogeneous context. The danger for Reed, however, as sometimes seems evident from his recent work, is that of self-caricature as a form of closure (fig. 5) via what I term the psychoaesthetic; that is, Reed's "religious" devotion to the strategies of Neo-Hoodooism may become automatic, repetitious, even self-

Figure 5
Creative "Apertures" and Risks of Closure

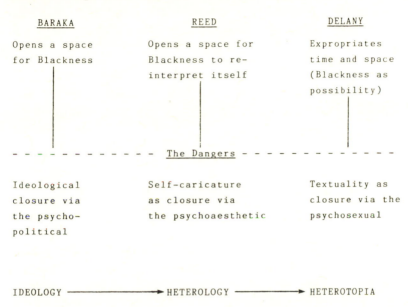

BARAKA	REED	DELANY
Opens a space for Blackness	Opens a space for Blackness to re-interpret itself	Expropriates time and space (Blackness as possibility)

- - - - - - - - - - - - The Dangers - - - - - - - - - - - - - - -

Ideological closure via the psycho-political	Self-caricature as closure via the psychoaesthetic	Textuality as closure via the psychosexual

IDEOLOGY ⟶ HETEROLOGY ⟶ HETEROTOPIA

parodying. (One recalls that the Yoruba Trickster, Èṣù, the "patron saint" as it were of Reed's enterprise, often makes mischief even in the context of otherwise positive activity.)

Delany has been devoted throughout his career to a vision of multiplexity, of pluralities of being (fig. 4). His priority has been to "texts," which I place in quotation marks to remind us that for Delany, as for a number of contemporary thinkers, text is something more than scripture; it is, indeed, akin to the ordering of experience. The business of blackness was never something Delany focused on as singularly or emphatically as did Baraka or Reed, but at the same time, by expropriating space and time in his future worlds in which black and other ethnic characters are situated, Delany was able to deal with blackness as possibility in a way that escaped both the ponderables of the past and the vagaries of the present (fig. 5). The problem that I discern as looming in his later work is one of textuality as closure via what I call the psychosexual, where the perception of an endless interplay between various sorts

of texts and insistent interpretations—an endless wheel of semiosis—becomes analogous to the compulsiveness of desire, the
polymorphous perversity of his (especially male) characters. Delany's emphasis on interpretation, combined with penetration (of
the body, of the unknown), yields what one might call a semi/er/
otic strategy.

The overall movement of the three writers within the context
of black American literature could be summarized as follows:
Baraka : IDEOLOGY → Reed : HETEROLOGY (the "science"
of otherness) → Delany : HETEROTOPIA (the radicalized
realm of possibilities) (fig. 5).

> On to . . . post new.
>
> Baraka, "Time Factor a Perfect Non-gap"

If Charles Newman is correct in his characterization of postmodernism as "ahistorical" (10), then I suggest that this is not the
case with black postmodernism. If Euro-American postmodernism
works against historicism, its Afro-American counterpart necessarily works in the direction of a different historical sense, one that
not only puts black back into the total historical view, but which
also (again necessarily) reexplores blackness in terms of itself. Similarly, when Newman claims a lack of "moral grounding" for postmodernism (26), an accusation I am not altogether sure is fully
justified but which, for the sake of argument, we will momentarily
accept as being consonant with his previous charge, I would again
have to differ with regard to Afro-American postmodernism,
which, while it may call into question conventional moral attitudes,
nevertheless has a strong ethical basis rooted in the demand for,
the need for, justice. It is impossible to read Jones/Baraka, Reed,
and Delany, for example, without recognizing that certain types
of behavior are being roundly castigated and other, alternative be-
haviors supported. Nowhere in the universe of black writing is
there such a thing as a purely amoral text.

Newman further characterizes our present reality as one of "a
multitude of competing discourses," "a genuine variety of inter-
cultural modes" (35), an "unprecedented multiplicity of voice" (33),

a "context of proliferating subcultures" (47), all of which he defines
as aspects of a "hyper-pluralism" (33) that is equatable in his view
to an essential valuelessness, a fragmentation of the cultural body
in which opinions are rife but knowledge is tenuous. However, a
genuine pluralism is not the same thing as factionalism or anomie,
with mutually hostile viewpoints all contending vigorously for ascendancy or at least a sufficiency of "exposure"; rather, true pluralism implies the simultaneity of diverse cultural experiences in a
circumstance of mutual respect and tolerance—a multicolored tapestry, not just a tangle of threads. Working backward from this
positive definition rather than Newman's negative one, Reed's characterization of the postmodern condition takes on a more com-
forting aspect, albeit an as yet unrealized one, for a situation of true
pluralism has still to emerge from the present-day jungle of dis-
parates. Reed wants to generate more momentum in this direction
of holism, whereas Newman believes things are already too inflated
and inflammatory.

What is being argued here is not that all experiences are equal,
but that each has its own validity. The American experience, after
all, is made up of many experiences. This is the essential point. I
am largely in agreement with Newman, Hal Foster, Suzi Gablik,
and others who believe postmodernism in the arts has not led automatically to greater freedom but indeed has opened many doors
to the "bad infinite" (Gablik, 11–12). Having acknowledged this,
I still insist that many so-called minority artists could legitimately
take up Artaud's cry, "No more masterpieces!"—not because they
are opposed to excellence but because they want to expunge the
presumptive superiority of canonized cultural icons of the self-
designated master class. This is what Reed and his cohorts are about.
Therefore, one understands the hostility toward pluralism ema-
nating from elitist quarters in society, for these are the people who
have a vested interest in mastership. On the other hand, the equal
hostility toward pluralism manifested by Marxists is explained by
the fact that they are eager to canonize the productions of another
class, the proletariat, designated as the final overturners of history.
The question of authority is central in both instances, and if postmodernism has gone too far in reacting to this, even putting its
own subversive "authority" under sharp and sardonic scrutiny, if
not erasure, this overthrow was, nevertheless, long overdue.

In the totalizing realm of late capitalism, with its appropriational and commodificational processes, perhaps it is only minority strategies that can offer an alternative, that can preserve spaces in which difference may operate. The semiotic field has not yet been colonized completely, especially in America, where subcultures are being replenished constantly by immigrants and refugees, and where, after four centuries, people of African origin still retain their own special identity. As Henry Louis Gates, Jr., reminds us, citing tradition, "Signification is the nigger's occupation" (685). Again, "The white folks got all the money, and [black folks] got all the signs" (Teish, 29).[3]

Notes

1. LeRoi Jones became Imamu Amiri Baraka in 1970; later, he dropped the title Imamu ("spiritual leader") but has retained his other names (which mean "blessed prince"). Since *The System of Dante's Hell* (1965) and *Tales* (1967) were written by LeRoi Jones, that is how I shall refer to him in my discussion of these works, which are my principal focus here, although I intend to put them into the perspective of the writer's overall career, especially in the postcultural-nationalist period. When I am speaking more generally, particularly in a contemporary context, I shall use the name Baraka, trusting the reader to understand that I am referring to a single individual who has, without understatement, gone through changes. Occasionally, I will have recourse to the compound Jones/Baraka—the form the man himself uses in the title of his 1984 autobiography—to indicate overlapping or transitional phases of his career.

2. Robert Hayden's reference to the past as a "soulscape" is perfectly apt for black cultural history's relationship to its origins (76). Traditionally, African time is synchronic; the present may extend into the near future but is mainly projected into the ancestral past (Anozie, 55, 57). It is the roots planted in that soulscape that nourish the spirit in the now.

3. Indeed, the Signifying Monkey of black folklore, so brilliantly examined by Gates, generally has the last laugh in the semiotic jungle. In Yoruba, òwè (monkey) and òwe (parable, proverb, riddle) are near homonyms. The Trickster plays with and on language and meaning, but words themselves are trickish and enable these permutations and "perversions."

2

LeRoi Jones/Amiri Baraka

A SCRIPTURE OF RHYTHMS

The System of Dante's Hell

Pound begins his *Cantos* with the conjunction "And," implying continuance; tradition and process are essentially uninterrupted, though we do not enter at the point of genesis. *The System of Dante's Hell* begins, significantly, with the word "But." Here, there is a taking exception to, a departure from, the known order. LeRoi Jones is working against tradition though deriving from it; this is the source of one of the principal tensions in his work.

For the oppressed, the past is always problematic. "History and tradition carry death; destruction is necessary; the color of hope is black." This statement by Vincent B. Leitch (66) is here recontextualized to make it speak from the perspective of the black artist. The first two clauses then will be understood to refer to white history and tradition as they have been imposed upon black people. An alternative unfolding is made implicit by the concluding clause; that is, that black history and tradition are preservative and salvational, providing the essential rhythms of black art. (The fact that a later dialogue with, and deconstruction of, that same black history and tradition eventually becomes possible and even desirable brings Leitch's statement back to something like its original intent. However, validation must come before reevaluation in the case of suppressed/oppressed bodies of circumstance and meaning.)

For Jones, Dante's hell is heaven because the pattern of judgment is going to be reversed (an emphasis we will find in Reed's work also) and because the symbolic descent into the underworld (and

the inferno of the self) results in a reemergence into positive blackness and beingness. Dante's hell is heaven, just as the Bottom is a
kind of funky paradise in *System*, just as essential blackness finally
offers redemption for Jones and for Ellison's Invisible Man before
him (for whom the universe has at last been inverted, thus making
it—for him as a black man—right side up).[1] Dante's hell is heaven,
again, because as two "monophonic" polarities they are inter-
changeable in a sense. Paradise, too, is monophonic (Zamyatin,
59), which is why it is well lost.[2] The Fall, the Tower of Babel—
these are sources of polyphony, of the mingled music of experience.

As I have suggested, the exhortation to see things in another light
necessarily embraces the Miltonic cosmos as well (Reed will invert
Milton as Jones inverts Dante). At issue is not only theology (Christianity as a justification of slavery) and order, or hierarchy, but
language. Stanley Fish's comment on the *"morality of stylistics"* in
Paradise Lost is very apt here:

> The poem embodies a Platonic aesthetic or anti-aesthetic in which the
> still clarity and white light of divine reality, represented (figured forth) in
> the atonal formality of God's abstract discourse, is preferred to the colour
> and chaotic liveliness of earthly motions, represented in Satan's "grand
> style" (88).

The distinction is between passionless and passionate language; between the lordly and the lowly; between sanctified and "devilish"
usage. Jones and Reed opt for the latter, "fallen" style—the language
of color, which is black vernacular—for, from a black perspective,
white language is the language of deceit. In the earliest Afro-American novel, William Wells Brown's *Clotel; or, The President's Daughter: A Narrative of Slave Life in the United States* (1853), after the
Reverend Snyder has tried ("in the atonal formality of God's abstract discourse") to convince a gathering of slaves that they must
obey their masters because "the Lord intended the negroes for
slaves," the slaves' conviction, when they are alone, is, " 'Dees
white fokes is de very dibble . . . and all dey whole study is to try
to fool de black people' " (74–75). White folks are the devil, and
white language is used perversely: this set of assumptions did not
originate with Black Muslims or the militant nationalists of the
1960s. (Indeed, the expression "white devils" occurs in Frank J.

Webb's *The Garies and Their Friends* [1857] and Charles W. Chest-
nutt's *The Marrow of Tradition* [1901], to cite two early literary
instances.) The other crucial point is that when we get really close
to black life in *Clotel*—as in the scene in the parson's kitchen (chapter
XII)—that life is rendered for the reader in the vernacular. Dante,
in *De Vulgari Eloquentia*, made a transition from a traditional level
of rhetoric to one that was highly idiomatic and uncompromised
by tradition (that is, the tradition of high culture rather than popular
culture). In a similar fashion, black expressive modes have survived
the dominational influence of white rhetoric.

It is for this reason that theorizing about forms of black discourse
can be vital not only for what it may disclose about black aesthetics
but equally for what it may reveal about cultural strategies, for the
speaking of a people is an index to its being. Despite the potency
of oral tradition, blacks early sought a "voice" in writing and "le-
gitimacy" in "standard" English. The privileging of the vernacular,
both as a nondeviant form of speech and as a valid literary medium,
took a long time, a lengthy struggle in which the natural voice of
black people had to assert itself beyond the street. As we shall see,
Reed's concept of Jes Grew seeking its text is a metaphor for the
quest of black language for an authentic literary expression. However, evidence of specifically black forms of knowing and revealing
can be traced even in the beginnings of the Afro-American literary
tradition.

Jones's hell begins with neutrality—that which neither is nor is
not; a lack of, or flight from, definition. In a universe of opposites
in conflict (black versus white, for example), there can be no real
safety or comfort in in-betweenness. Shades of grey are just that:
shades—ghosts or illusions—symbolizing nonbeing or death.
(Jones/Baraka's entire career has been one of ongoing redefinition,
and always it has been away from, or against, an established ideal
or circumstance; in other words, it has been consistently dialectical.
Neutrality suspends the dialectic; there is no movement, only a
deathlike stasis, or else any appearance of motion is obscured, as
in a fog.)

Blue is the first color we encounter in *System*, and it is the color
used most frequently in the novel, followed closely, predictably
enough, by black and white. Blue is found across the spectrum of
meaning in Jones's work, from the blues as a metaphysical condition

and art form all the way to the extraterrestrial blue men who make their appearance at the end of *Tales*.

The shifting color symbolism is important, for we are called upon here to alter our vision, to invest our minds with a new way of seeing. The new light of revelation is actually a darkness; enlightenment, for the "colored" man, lies in recomprehending his blackness, which yields for him exact definition. Prior to this movement of consciousness, everything appears grey—the color of the vestibule of the Inferno, the color that oppression takes on when it reduces the oppressed person to a psychological status of nonentity or invisibility.

A significant aspect of hell is systematization. There is an overpowering sense of inevitability, of things locked into place, "DISPOSED OF" (64). The fact that the narrator in the novel is often running dramatizes his efforts to break out, but this image also emphasizes the treadmill-like nature of his efforts. The transcendence of this imprisonment, of the ghetto of the self as well as the ghetto of false, externally imposed definition, begins with an understanding akin to that of Invisible Man at the conclusion of Ellison's novel when he recognizes that in his long and complex journey through the matrix of black experience, he has been able to confront and finally surmount everything but the mind. Historically, the black man was able to find advantage in the realization that whatever the power of the oppressor, "he don't know my mind." However, knowing one's own mind, and harmonizing that deep self-knowledge with one's true needs and desires, is a necessary next step toward freedom. Neutrals have not been able to take this step; they are unfocused, misdirected.

When the narrator in "Heathen: No. 2" refers to "myself, who had not yet become beautiful" (20), he does not mean what later Mr. Bush means when he admonishes his student charges (in Ray McGhee's "reading" of his message) not to "act like that word. Don't fail us. We've waited for all you handsome boys too long" (*Tales*, 16). The word, unspoken, is "nigger," implying everything the black bourgeoisie (like Invisible Man) is fleeing from. However, in this basically integrationist period—to borrow a phrase Ayi Kwei Armah employed as the title of his first novel—"the beautyful ones are not yet born," and they will not be until they can escape the white definition of "nigger" and embrace, and then assert, the essential soulness that it implies from a black perspective. Again, as in the case of Invisible Man, there must be an acceptance of the legacy of all those "black years" behind the broken or worn faces of the people (*Tales*, 1), that hidden, collective history beneath the personal. The narrator of *System* has to advance beyond "the bare period of my desires" when there was "Nothing to interest me but myself" (14–15). Commitment finally replaces desire or, perhaps more accurately, becomes the vehicle merging desire and the self. The invisible (blue/s) man who dwells in grey neutrality will eventually emerge militant, sharply defined. The movement is one which proceeds from negation to affirmation.

The narrator declares, "Who writes this will never read it" (59). One reason is that writing is a process of alteration/transformation; in a word, metamorphosis. "Loup Garou means change into," writes Reed (*Chattanooga*, 49). The worker-in-language works changes all the time, writing out of him/herself in at least a double sense, as Rimbaud acknowledged when he declared, "Je est un Autre." However, *System* and *Tales* are also an exorcism of the "darkness" of too much whiteness (the "brilliance" that casts a harsh shadow over the oppressed), prefatory to the redemptive descent into blackness, with its simultaneous ascent of consciousness. These tales are not for repetition; they are testimonies of "heresy, against one's own sources" (*System*, 7)[3]—the sin of Invisible Man—of a tormented progress toward "the next level of vision" (*Tales*, 118). In the process, Dante, *Uncle Tom's Cabin*, Horatio Alger, and such, are all radically revised or done to death. There is a violent restructuring—or deconstruction—of the mythography of America and of the West in general. In this sense and to this extent Jones is akin to Reed; where he differs—and drastically—is in the nature of his substitutions, his alternatives.

As he writes in "The Prodigal," Jones is searching for his own "Vita Nuova," a new life through which he will be transformed. He says in one of his essays, "Newark St. years later—Dante vanished, a Black Man in his place" (*Raise Race Rays Raze: Essays Since 1965*, 49). To achieve this, his protagonist must "Push towards (SOME END" (*System*, 64). Here, the words "illustrate" the sense: the END is bigger than the means. The end is blackness, a black world. The means is a transvaluation of value from Eurocentric to Afrocentric, a consolidation of energies to feed a gathering momentum.

In fact, "Pure movement" (*System*, 32) is what Jones is seeking and what his language evokes. (The metaphysics of blackness has to do with movement and continuity.) However, it is not the movement of, for example, Jack Kerouac's "bop prosody," which is as breathless and unpunctuated as the road itself; rather, it is an urban prose of jerky rhythms, full of starts and stops. It emphasizes the phrase, staccato notes, whereas Kerouac's line is more melodic, based more on the sentence or even the paragraph. I would analogize Kerouac's typewriter to George Shearing's piano, Jones's to Lester Young's saxophone. Music, at any rate, is key, especially black music, with its expressive freedom: "Rhythm. Passports" (*System*, 70).

Black literature, indeed, aspires above all to the condition of black music. It always desires to go beyond the dull word to something electrifying. There are blue words in black writing, just as there are blue notes in jazz. Jones and Reed write books, but what dances between the covers derives as much from other media (especially radio and cinema) as it does from literary tradition, although it is worth emphasizing that black literary tradition is founded to a large extent upon "blue speech" (*System*, 38), the oral tradition which is itself closely allied to music.

Claude McKay's stories—to take the example of one writer who needs to be more widely read—document this very well. Consider the following few lines from *Gingertown* (1932): " 'Come on, buddies,' said the mulatto. 'We may be suckers all right in Rosie's joint, but we won't be suckers in a cat dog bite mah laig hear the player piano crying fair chile baby oh boy house' " (69). The last seventeen words offer an early analogue for the kind of language Reed employs in his writings. In McKay's oeuvre this kind of riff stands out like an unexpected chord change, compared to its pervasiveness in Reed or the git-down raps of the Black Arts poets. Similarly, while McKay and other authors of the pre–Second Renaissance period often refer to music ("Blues. Pianola blues, gramophone blues. Easy-queasy, daddy-mammy, honey-baby, brown-gal, black-boy, hot-dog blues" [148]), by the time we get to the 1960s, the music has become part of the language itself to a far more conspicuous degree than even McKay's occasional tight-like-that phrasing seems to suggest was possible. (He knew it was possible; so did Paul Laurence Dunbar. However, the pressures exerted by a "mainstream" audience kept the vernacular "in its place." Consider the code-switching that is indulged in in chapter IV of Frank Webb's *The Garies and Their Friends*, where Ben puts on the slave dialect when he tries to play upon the presumed sympathies of Mr. Winston, a mulatto whom he mistakes for a southern gentleman, but otherwise talks "correct English" [Webb's phrase, 38–40].) Delany's work, contrastingly, sometimes seems to aspire to the level of high tech, in theory as well as practice.

Jones acknowledged Creeley, Olson, Snyder, Ginsberg, and O'Hara as early influences (Hudson, 58), but it is Creeley in particular who appears to have had the most profound impression on Jones's fiction. Creeley, of course, is best known as a major figure in contemporary poetry, but he initially saw himself as primarily a prose writer, and his first collection of fiction, *The Gold Diggers*, was published in 1954. Jones knew and appreciated Creeley's work; he included half a dozen of Creeley's stories and the preface to *The Gold Diggers* in his 1963 anthology, *The Moderns*. Furthermore, Creeley was closely associated with Charles Olson, who was an influence on Jones's early literary theory as well as practice, and on Creeley's dictum, quoted with approval by Jones (introduction to *The Moderns*, xvi), that "Form is no more than an extension of content."

The style evidenced in pieces like Creeley's "Three Fate Tales" or "The Seance" (originally published in 1951) would appear to provide a very close analogue to Jones's own prose style. Consider the following passage:

I used to live in the city, in the middle of it, straight, tall buildings, some of it, but where I was they were cramped, squat, four stories. There was a trolley line ran down the middle of the street. Noise. . . .
  Thinking of that time, as it comes here, here and now, I think of the other, somewhat different. I say time. I say time, to mean place (Creeley, 32).

There is a remarkable likeness here between the tone of Creeley's writing, controlled yet a bit enervated, his rhythms, with their frequently short phrasing and subtle repetitions, and Jones's writing in *System* and *Tales*.

Although Baraka now claims that in writing *System* he was "tear-ing away from the 'ready-mades' that imitating Creeley (or Olson) provided" (*Autobiography*, 166), similarities remain; yet they are not the essential thing, given the exchanges of influence between white and black artists. Jazz, anyway, in its various permutations, un-derlies if not instigates all of these discourses.

The concept of ready-mades derives from Dadaism—precisely, from Marcel Duchamp, who in the role of artist-as-critic was raising serious questions about the nature of art in an increasingly object-ridden society. Art no longer seemed "natural," and Dada sought to liberate it from elitism and specialization. It is not without cun-ning that LeRoi Jones entitled one of his most powerful poems "Black Dada Nihilismus." The title is a specimen of a positive kind of "mumbo jumbo" that connects with the jabberwocky conspiracy Reed promotes and participates in; it is a "spell" designed to liberate the black consciousness from its white nightmare. This liberation proceeds in part from a recognition and reembrace of the ready-mades of Afro-American culture, of which the blues impulse is one preeminent example. "Black Dada Nihilismus" annihilates white influences and celebrates the ancestral roots of the black heritage. Consequently, another source or analogy that could be invoked as a stylistic influence on Jones's prose is what Robert Farris Thomp-son has referred to as "African staccato plastic form" (37). The textual "roughness" and complexity of *System* and *Tales* is com-parable to the textural roughness and complexity of a good deal of African sculpture.

"In Chicago I kept making the queer scene," the narrator tells us in "Grafters" (57). His bisexuality is akin to his biracialism: he is split down the middle. When Jones advances to his cultural-nationalist position, these forms of ambiguity become intolerable. A choice is necessary: one must choose manhood or lose it alto-gether; one must choose blackness or lose one's soul. It is in this period that "faggots" are put down in Jones's writings, and al-though he has subsequently engaged in self-criticism with regard to this and other expressions of bigotry, the fact that he was then most influential has tended to lock many of his critics onto the statements he uttered at that time, even though they were only one manifestation of what he himself has called "my perpetual-motion mouth," one stage in the "travailing motion from me to me" (*Au-*

tobiography, 10, 68). Cheryl Clarke, for example, in "The Failure to Transform: Homophobia in the Black Community," attacks Jones as "a rabid homophobe" as well as a sexist and cites his poetry and essays to support her condemnation (201). She seems unaware of the gay aspects of the fiction or of the sympathetic portrait of the homosexual as victim in *The Toilet*. It is very likely that the general homophobia of the black community and the macho stance of Black Power combined to energize Jones's abandonment of the homoerotic element; nevertheless, homosexuality is still an important metaphor in *System* in "The Eighth Ditch (Is Drama," dealing with fraudulent counsellors. It is a crucial section which, significantly, comes at the very middle of the book.

There are two main characters: 46, who represents the narrator of *System* as a youth and who also resembles the Boy in *The Baptism*, and 64, who is like the Homosexual in that play. There is a sense in which 64 is a future aspect of 46; their complementarity is symbolized in their sexual union. 46 is "dead america"; he is also "myself, who has not yet come out" (79).

64 is damned; he is in hell because he is poor and black. (46 is also damned, but he does not yet realize it, being too caught up in false elegance.) 64 is The Street, "a maelstrom of definitions" (80)—those things which the middleclass black youth is afraid of, and which, like the Bottom later on, he flees. 64 violates 46 because he wants him to remember him and what he represents: black struggle, black suffering—not Romantic ennui. 46 thinks that he will become pregnant, and the consequence of this (which he cannot yet foresee) is that he will give birth to himself anew.

It is not 64 who is a false counsellor, but the others whom 46 has been heeding who have been conditioning him to love the middleclass, to be an imitation white person. With the pride of youth, 46 thinks that he knows a great deal, but 64 warns him that his presumptive knowledge is only superficial. 46 may believe he is slick, but 64 tells him, "I know things that will split your face" (83).

46 is the leader of the Secret Seven and, later, of the New Group. However, they are treacherous; they commit rape. The narrator calls them a New Order and says that they turned to him for guidance, but at the same time he seems contemptuous of them for taking his own "stupid trials . . . as axioms" (108).

A New Order has already been referred to in the novel, in a

description of the violence perpetrated by black gangs. The narrator calls it totalitarianism, which is dual in nature: black people oppressed by the white power structure (neo-slavery) and black people subjected to terrorism by elements of their own community (what Reed calls the plague of Louisiana Red).

In creating his own New Order, the narrator has established a private species of totalitarianism. In another important section of the novel, "The Rape," he describes his own mercilessness when the woman they contemplate raping (an actual damned soul who suffers from torments the narrator and his companions are insulated from; like 64, she is The Street) tells them she has venereal disease. He refuses to countenance any cop-outs and attempts to rally his "troops" against the "enemy," completely failing to realize that he is the enemy. In this victimization of a victim, they are all conspiring against their own actual reality, not the one they have imagined. In this assault on black womanhood, they are implicating themselves in the ugly ethos of slavery, becoming participants in the very horrors from which they seek to flee.

This negative historical continuity is reiterated in the final section of the novel when the narrator refers to the woman who has just left the juke-joint (with his friend Don) as Don's "property" (130). She is a weekend whore (the text makes it clear that these young women are prostituting themselves to escape from poverty) and has "sold" herself for the night, but the concept of human property is so essentially tied to the practice of slavery that we cannot possibly read the word in any limited, ahistorical sense. Jones wants us to understand that if slavery is over, the psychology of slavery remains and is operative even in its former victims, the ex-slaves. (Reed also focuses on this phenomenon, particularly in *The Last Days of Louisiana Red* and *Flight to Canada*.)

In retrospect, the narrator recoils from this former self, whom he refers to as "Hideous magician!" Rejecting all that he has sought as a young man (elegance, middleclass values, "whiteness"), Jones embraces the opposite. He breaks out of his elliptical orbit and becomes one of "the advanced."

The final section of *System*, "The Heretics," is the longest single piece in the novel and the most straightforwardly written. The narrator descends into the Bottom, the black community of Shreveport, Louisiana (which is near the literal bottom of America). He goes there having already been trapped by images (of beauty, of whiteness) and is caught up temporarily in those "wordless energies" (121) which permeate the black experience and which later were to have such an important effect on Jones's life and art.

Here, however, he has reached the nadir of his descent into the Inferno and is so far divorced from his roots that he can say of the inhabitants of the bottom, "They live in blackness" (122) and mean this (from his perspective then) in the pejorative sense created by white definition. He can say, "I hate coons" (123) and mean it because his own view of himself is entirely different. ("We stood . . . huge *white* men who knew the world" [125]; my emphasis.) To the black youths who accost him toward the end, he is "Mr. Half-white muthafucka" (151).

Homosexuality comes into play again to underscore the narrator's vulnerability as well as his confusion. His acknowledgment of "an actual longing for men" (129) precedes his encounter with Peaches, a young prostitute, who later accuses him of being a sissy and not liking women, but who is also determined, in her own way, to make a "man" out of him. This struggle culminates in an image of emasculation tied to release. Peaches is manipulating him in order to make him have an erection: "(She was pulling too hard now & I thot everything would give and a hole in my stomach would let out words and tears)" (139–40). This suggests not only an emotional catharsis but an intellectual one. His (false) knowledge has stood in the way of his understanding; he needs to learn the lesson articulated even before the novel properly begins that feeling precedes belief (7). This uncartesian epistemology, which one might term neo-negritude, begins to strike the narrator with full force in the juke-joint, when he enters into the "rite" of the dance with Peaches. "I danced. And my history was there" (129). He still intellectualizes and ironizes the experience, as is his studied habit, but he remains entangled in the flux of those wordless energies, so that his imagined emasculation, when it comes (cutting him off, so to speak, from his past sins), seems to bring a sharp revelation: "This was the world. . . . A real world, of flesh, of smells, of soft black harmonies and color" (148). He thereafter falls—temporarily—into an easy, natural life-style, but he cannot escape his essential cowardice, which is his old fear of yielding to blackness. Turning away from what he needs but cannot yet embrace, he leaves

Peaches, leaves the Bottom, ascending from the white-labeled hell (his unrecognized, or unaccepted, heaven) toward that heaven which is, in the end, the black man's hell.

Vengeance is swift in coming, arriving at the hands of a trio of ghetto youth offended by his false slickness. They beat him; they then seem to hold a phantasmagorical wake for him, and he is resurrected, born again, within the cave/womb, to a realm of new possibility. Whether or not he seizes this chance to redeem himself depends on which god he is calling upon for assistance: the God of Dante's heaven or a "lost god Damballah." The coda, "Sound and Image," leaves little doubt as to the ultimate answer, which is that salvation can come only through recourse to a stronger imagery more indigenous to the Afrocentric consciousness. This is the "end" of the novel, but it is the starting point for a plunge into black sources, into a quest for what Cuban poet Palés Matos has called "the essence of the black model" (Cartey, 97).

Tales

Tales opens with "A Chase (Alighieri's Dream)." We are back in the Inferno, Dante's—and Jones's—System. We are in the midst again of brokenness. Identity and consciousness are shattered, but so is the locale, the human/geographic anchorage. Nothing any longer is whole.

The book appears to have two "movements." The first nine stories generally parallel the odyssey depicted in *System*, filling in some of the spaces that were left blank on that black pointillist canvas. In fact, the last story in the first grouping in *Tales*, "Salute," deals with an incident that occurred while Jones was serving in the air force, the same time period in which "The Heretics" takes place (around 1954–1956).[4] Beginning with "Words," the first tale in the second grouping, he has moved up to Harlem (1965). The intervening period is represented by only two pieces which, typically, do not fall into their proper place chronologically in the book's structure. These are "Going Down Slow" and "Heroes Are Gang Leaders."

"Heroes" begins with the narrator sitting in a hospital bed and reading, surrounded by derelicts. He is looking for an answer to the question of how to make the "wildest, brightest dispersal of our energies" (64). He insists on the need for a philosophy which will give coherence to both the individual and the collective effort, but this philosophy, for Jones, has tended to translate as ideology, with the ever-present danger of becoming prescriptive rather than inspirational.

In what he calls "the essay part" of the story, Jones shows his persona retreating into a novel about "the pursuit of heroism" as a way of avoiding an act of real personal heroism on a minor level (that is, keeping the cops from harassing his ward neighbor, Kowalski). Literature is intended to take the blame for this evasion, but if the book's lessons are sound, who *is* actually to blame for the failure to meld thought to action? Heroes, we are told, are gang leaders. Action is a collective thing, opposed to the solitary pursuit of literature. Yet collective action too often precludes personal responsibility; it becomes mob action. Individual behavior is still important, and the narrator's failure in the tale is an individual one, which cannot be blamed on books.

It is interesting that this story follows "Going Down Slow," the most straightforward narrative in *Tales*, in which an individual act is carried out by the protagonist, Lew Crosby (LeRoi Jones), that is both cowardly and unjustified. Crosby has been having an affair with another woman and not only denies it but is outraged to discover that his wife has slept with the Japanese painter Mauro. Not only is his condemnation of his wife hypocritical—a typical sexist stance—but he allows his jealousy (probably doubly charged by guilt) to turn into violence, brutally assaulting Mauro, then anesthetizing himself with heroin as an escape from the unstable network of relationships he inhabits.

In "The Alternative," the narrator recognizes that he inhabits a country "of thought" (7). He must travel from this (white) space to a (black) nation of feeling, advance from "Dead ends" to living means. His companions are like "floating empty nouns" (11)—people without connection to anything truly meaningful, only to a reiterated, sought-after, but essentially irrelevant "culture" which they all want to possess and to whose precepts they are trying to conform. However, the "floating empty nouns" are also aspects of a language without authenticity, a white language of false elegance that is simply the wrong style for the black artist whose themes are black.

This piece deals with Jones's student days at Howard University. He is still a leader, though blinded by his own failure of consciousness and surrounded by (moral, spiritual) death. As before, in his earlier days of gangsmanship, his position as leader is based upon intellection and verbal skills, not physical strength.

Here, the leader's name is Ray (the same as the protagonist in *The Toilet*, who is also called Foots), though at least once he is referred to as Everett (13), which is Jones's actual first name. His companions go upstairs to harass another student, Hutchens, who is being visited by a middle-aged homosexual named Lyle, while Ray remains behind, "shivering at his crimes" (23). Like Ray in *The Toilet*, who sneaks back afterward to comfort the battered James Karolis, he is afraid to show his true self to these "dead souls, I call my people" (22). Jones sees his college friends as having been corrupted by the apostles of assimilation, who admonish them to adhere to the white man's ways as a means of achieving middleclass respectability and a commensurate degree of acceptance into the white world. His friends, he tells us, become lawyers and teachers, while he alone is left "without cause or place." He finds both through the advocacy of blackness, speaking scathingly, from his new level of consciousness, of "That way. Which, now, I sit in judgment of" (11).

The evil fiction of false masculinity (cf. "Going Down Slow") and the arrogant persecution of "peasants" by the middleclass are symbolized by the other students' harassment of Hutchens and Lyle. Ray finally goes upstairs and sees the future champions of the black bourgeoisie engaged in an ugly parody of a lynching, the awful irony of which is underscored by the fact that their victims are black like themselves, a ritual that strongly suggests they are really attacking their own latent insecurities (recall my remarks concerning the inconclusive rape in *System*). Ray attempts to stop them and is knocked down against the "protestant" floor (29). He has brutally confronted the Protestant Ethic, profit and loss (his friends have gained a world but lost their *soul*), the values that transform people into "rich famous butcher[s]." The alternative to all this (hence the title) is a rejection of such values.

In order to escape from the fateful irony of the "noble" life for which college is ostensibly preparing him, Jones has to immerse himself in "The Largest Ocean in the World," which is night (blackness) or consciousness. (One thinks of Conrad's admonition in *Lord Jim*, exploiting the same metaphor: "In the destructive element immerse.") His equilibrium has been destroyed. He walks "near the theaters, where the city changed" (33), a literal image but also a metaphoric one suggestive of drama as a ritualizing and revolutionizing mode. When he presses himself against the darkness and lets it "sink in" (33), it is not only a sexual image relating to the androgynous transformation which takes place in the final paragraph; it also describes the passionate embrace of a new (black) consciousness. The whole piece, indeed, is a tone poem describing metamorphosis, the "drowning" of one self and the "birth" of another.

The concept of metamorphosis is central in all three of the authors under scrutiny here, but what is really at issue is consciousness, for if that does not change there is no change. Ellison's Invisible Man goes through many shifts of identity (student, factory worker, agitator, and so on) but is still left struggling with the mind, and Reed parodies this incomplete dialectic through the character of Bukka Doopeyduk in *The Freelance Pallbearers*. Bron Helstrom, in Delany's novel *Triton*, can alter his gender (even his race, if he wished), but he remains untransformed in terms of his psychological being. The quest for a real alteration of consciousness seems to have energized a good deal of American writing right from the beginning. (Crèvecoeur claimed that the American was a new breed, but his statement implies much more than the actuality.) Today, people talk of going through "changes," but one of the frustrations facing those of the old or new transcendental persuasion is the way in which the more things change in America, the more they remain the "same." The urgency for real change probably has been greater among black people because their situation has been so radically difficult. If the fact of slavery in this country has severely tested the ideal of liberty, the postemancipation existence of blacks has been an index of the constantly receding nature of this ideal and its perpetual inconclusiveness.

In "The Death of Horatio Alger," the narrator, here called Mickey, wants to "Rise and Slay" (43), like Black Dada Nihilismus, the vengeful spirit that will rise in "the smoking hells of soon to be destroyed Yankee Gomorrahs" (44). This is another instance of the exorcising, sanitizing power of violence (rhetorical and actional), as well as an allusion to the conjuring of new forces that will replace the negative possession by old (imposed) ones. (This latter idea is what Reed's Neo-Hoodooism is all about. Reed, though, insists that in the deepest historical sense these "new" forces are really the most ancient ones, coming around again to liberate us from the oppressive tendencies of Pl/atonism.)

The relationship between possession and dispossession can be seen very well in "The Screamers," one of Jones's best pieces of writing, which centers around the experience of a performance by a Newark saxophonist named Lynn Hope. Jones focuses on the distinctive sound of Hope's playing, which emphasizes a "repeated rhythmic figure, a screamed riff, pushed in its insistence past music" (76). It is uncompromising, a perfect specimen of negritude that "reinforced the black cults of emotion" (76). Through music, the performer becomes both an ethnic historian and a priest of the unconscious, while the jazz performance itself is a ritual enactment. Although Hope is blowing his own individual expression, his honking is holistic, a communal statement linking the audience together and leading them out into the night, into action. Jones writes: "It would be the form of the sweetest revolution, to hucklebuck into the fallen capital, and let the oppressors lindy-hop out" (79). This sounds like a revolution engineered by Jes Grew or the Loop Garoo Kid; it is Yellow Back Radio tuned in to a Third World station.

The concluding piece to *Tales*, "Answers in Progress," has been called "Black Power science fiction" (Lacey, 193). It deals with a successfully ongoing black revolution, in the midst of which spaceships land piloted by extraterrestrials anxious to pick up on the latest jazz sides. Significantly, the spacemen are colored (blue); they are blues people, possessed of perfect harmony that extends beyond the musical. Sun Ra is one of the musicians invoked here; he is of particular importance because of his visionary sensibility, his name—which refers to the Kemetic (ancient Egyptian) origins of black civilization and which equally suggests the stellar—and his instrumentality in bringing black music into the space age.[5]

The violence which Jones here posits as part of the Answer may be very much of this world, but it is played out to a cosmic soundtrack. Indeed, the appearance of the blue space "cats" lends a powerful dose of surrealism to the revolution, undercutting its seeming matter-of-factness with some alien high jinks. However, the fact that it is an art form (jazz) which can unite this world with other worlds reveals that the true revolution is cultural (cf. "The Screamers").

If one accepts Werner Sollors's schema of the four phases of Jones/Baraka's changing commitments (8), the writing of *System* falls within the second phase, of ethnopolitical protest, and the writing of *Tales* comes within the third phase, of cultural nationalism. However, the essential energy linking these two works—which recount and reevaluate his life up to that time—is a relentless momentum deeper into blackness. These fugitive narratives describe the harried flight of an intensely self-conscious Afro-American artist/intellectual from the neo-slavery of blinding, neutralizing whiteness, where the arena of struggle is basically within the mind.[6] This is precisely the pattern of *Invisible Man*, of which Jones's *System* may be seen as a "deconstructed" version.[7]

Jones's *System*, to use Henry Louis Gates, Jr.'s, favorite trope, signifies upon Dante and Western metaphysics, as well as upon the black *Bildungsroman* as neo-slave narrative. For Jones, the black man cannot be "saved" by entering the white paradise through either guidance or guile. His *Autobiography* documents his growing up in "a maze of light and darkness," "always in motion" (1), among "the black running masses" (13), a recapitulation of the circumstances and imagery of *System* and *Tales*, where the past is recalled in scattered impressions of youth and fragments of a lost wholeness, combined with a sought-after fulfillment that *lies* (is situated in / is potentially deceiving) in the future. The (en)forced coherence of the Western worldview can only represent incoherence to a dominated people of different cultural origins, which is why Jones conjoins "histories and rhythms" (*Tales*, 73). There are rhythms to history, but there are also different histories of rhythm. Black people have their own: a different coherence. Musicians are priests of the psyche who talk of, with, spirits. Saxophonists are *griots*; their horns speak. The drums talk, too—talk through—reminding us that the "New Spirit" is at the same time very ancient. As stated in *Kawaida Studies*: "The actual *beginnings* of our expression are post Western (just as they are certainly pre-western)" (32).

... & After

If one wished to crudely compartmentalize Baraka's work, the poems could be seen as attacks; the essays as justifications; the plays as "demonstrations"; and the fiction as self-analysis and exorcism. I have endeavored to show that *System* and *Tales* offer enormous insight into the psychohistory of a complex and extremely influential personality; for this reason alone, it would be intriguing to know what the long, still unpublished novel Baraka wrote after *Tales*, and which he himself describes as a failure, is about (Sollors, 257–258).

In any event, Baraka's recent piece of short fiction, "Blank" (1985), certainly represents no advance on the work he was doing in this genre in the 1960s; on the contrary, it indicates something of a deadening. The blankness exists not only in the mind of the protagonist, a wealthy man who suddenly loses his memory ("he did not know anything but the surfaces of things" [287]), but inheres as well in the telling of the tale. When Baraka writes that his character experiences "Words without substance with invisible contexts" (287), this is a fitting description of the story itself, for the reader knows little more than does this man, who suffers from unaccounted-for amnesia (if that is his problem; his thought, "I am in darkness with no road in or out" [287] suggests something more sinister or metaphysical); it is also the precise opposite of the kind of language Whitman celebrated in "Song of Myself," word-music that would embody "Nature without check with original energy" (note the syntactic parallelism with Baraka's statement)—the same kind of natural-born evocation that black speech and black literature so often have displayed. What is natural, real, has become artificial, abstract.

The man is rich; his very presence commands deference. His company is named Close Securities, but he himself is not secure, for first he forgets who he is, and then at the end he is abruptly accosted by his black chauffeur, Scales (of Justice?). His company produces, among other things, information, but it is precisely information, even of an elementary kind, that he no longer possesses (and which the reader also lacks, due to "invisible contexts"). Or perhaps the problem is that he is suffering from a surfeit of data. After all, this is supposed to be the Information Age, but the irony is that in our own society the ever-increasing glut of information has not only failed to do away with ignorance, indeed, it has generated new forms of ignorance, new forms of anxiety. Privacy and silence are becoming rarer. Perhaps the amnesia of Baraka's protagonist is a defense against the terminality of information overload. The quest for meaning may involve the accumulation of data, but too much data can become meaningless; too much input may override consciousness. Then the subconscious may take control. Scales, then, symbolizes the release of the repressed; the indecision of the ruling elite facilitates action on the part of the underdog, whose "information" is more elementary and survival-oriented.

Obviously, this piece is intended as an anticapitalist parable, but it seems strangely self-implicating because it is as foreclosed, sterile, blank as the consciousness it seeks to indict.

The imaginatively circumscribed nature of Baraka's work over the past decade would seem to necessitate a reconsideration of black cultural nationalism and the Black Arts movement, which have had their most profound and lasting influence in the revolutionizing of creativity, rather than in the creation of revolution. Previously unattempted political strategies seem harder and harder to find; meanwhile, black experience is being articulated, analyzed, and revisioned in black literature with greater genius than ever before.

The novel often was disparaged in the Black Arts period as an inappropriate vehicle for the immediate concerns of the revolution. Radical concerns in contemporary Africa have led some writers and critics to a similar questioning of the novel's relevance as a weapon in the struggle against neo-colonialism. The novel, however, demands much, offers much; it resists reification. Perhaps this militant bias against the novel has been fortunate for the genre, which has avoided a good deal of the stridency and didacticism manifest in a significant number of poems and dramas. Black literature first found its voice in prose—in the slave narratives—and it is in prose today that the psyche of black people, the poignancy and lyricism of black life, are being most completely and most powerfully rendered.

Certain of Baraka's recent criticisms of cultural nationalism are valid, especially with regard to its sometimes confused adoption of African imagery and the reactionary nature of some of its doctrines, but I believe his total rejection of cultural nationalism as a backward posture is mistaken. Nationalism as a form of exclusivism is, ultimately, a negative ideology, though at certain vital moments of a people's or a country's history it may be a positive stance, even a necessary one. Black cultural nationalism now has largely passed through that stage, but while separatism no longer may be the primary goal, the concept of a black nation is not thereby rendered untenable. The fact is the black nation as a cultural entity does exist and has for a long time. Cultural nationalism implies recognition of this truth and the consequent need to retain the integrity and vitality of cultural forms. There is always the danger in America that so-called mainstream culture (which is really an anticulture) will render authentic cultural forms impotent through expropriation or mimicry, though black Americans have traditionally survived this process by means of a dynamic of continuous creation sustained by the taproots of their complex heritage (what Baraka in another context calls "the changing same," an expression I have already had recourse to in this work because of its aptness). A corollary to this is the recognition of how much of what is taken for granted as American culture has its origins in blackness (as a mode of being). Euro-American culture has extended and reanimated itself constantly by parasitically drawing upon Afro-American culture.

Baraka uses such terms as "submissionist," "capitulationist," and "comprador" to characterize black artists and intellectuals who do not share his own radical precepts. Though he admits that the majority of Afro-American writers may be described as "middle forces," Baraka nevertheless insists that "the genuine, major Afro-American writers have been part of the revolutionary tradition" (*Daggers and Javelins: Essays, 1974–1979*, 310). However, his definition of "revolutionary" rests on solely political grounds, a definition too narrow to embrace all the "genuine, major" black authors. It is worthwhile noting Herbert Read's statement: "A tradition in art is not a body of beliefs: it is a knowledge of techniques." Complementary to this is Stravinsky's opinion that "revolution is one thing, innovation another" (Mitchell, 21, 64).

The ideological struggle over what should be the "authentic" tradition of Afro-American writing is interesting and stimulating but ultimately dangerous because it is analogous to the restrictive, exclusivist sense of tradition established by white critics over the years with regard to American literature.[8] Reed's complaint about the authoritarianism of One Tradition has been validated by the present pluralogue concerning canons under way in academia, and having battled against such chauvinism directed against blacks and other minorities by whites, Reed was unlikely to countenance such treatment directed against blacks by blacks. Reed consistently has argued that single traditions are distortions unless they encompass all ranges of experience. The disparagement of writers and thinkers as illegitimate on ideological grounds is a serious error that does a disservice not only to art but to the broader dimensions of Afro-American reality. Unity is not necessarily homogeneity, but Baraka's hostility to what he calls "individualism" logically limits diversity. There is, no doubt, a myth of the self under capitalism, but socialist ideology has propagated a countermyth of collectivity which is certainly hard to evidentiate in a positive and concrete manner in the modern world.

The revolutionary tradition of black Americans which Baraka and others speak of has always found its most vital and persistent expression in the arts, especially music. It advocates freedom, change, roots, and it is not materialistic in orientation. This may help to explain why works like *A Black Mass* and *Slaveship* are so much more powerful and effective as art than works like *The Motion of History*, when all three are so clearly polemical. The former dramas derive from the (pre-Baraka) early cultural-nationalist phase, the latter from the Marxist–Leninist–Maoist (M–L–M) phase, and this appears to provide the key, rather than any serious diminution of power or skill on Baraka's part. The Marxist work is intellectually determined, whereas the cultural-nationalist pieces are emotionally felt. For Baraka—indeed, for the majority of artists and intellectuals in America—the international capitalist/communist struggle must remain an abstraction in a way that it can never be for our counterparts in the Third World. Racism, on the other hand, is experienced far more concretely. *The Motion of History* and many of Baraka's recent poems display too overtly a materialist skeleton hung with the papier-mâché of ideology, while *Slaveship*, contrastingly, is a ritual reenactment, an historical communion.

The strength of successful works of a socialist orientation derives not from the persuasiveness of their informing ideology but rather from their energy of opposition, the power of their portrayal of injustice—precisely those virtues which characterize many non-socialist protest writings. However, the studied polemic, the doctrinal script are always inferior to those works in which the political import is broadly fused with imaginative power—in which we are compelled by life, not lectures. A polemical and polarizing ideology can never lead us out of the "labyrinth of history" or navigate us safely around the "confusing land-masses of myth" (Harris, 23, 58).

In his cultural-nationalist period, Baraka sought to blacken the zero of white values and to make that hermeneutical circle, unrevealing of black experience, a rooted sphere through the added dimension of a "spirit reach." Excessively ritualized and mythologized, the black value system then espoused still had the virtue of organizing black energies in reconstructive channels. However, in Baraka's latest phase, designated by the alphabetical incantation M–L–M, the ceremonialized, celebrative sphere is flattened once more into an arena of materialist conflict (fig. 6).

If one desires an antidote to Baraka's Marxist rhetoric derived from a black perspective, one could profitably turn to Richard Wright's *American Hunger* (1944). By making a significant individual contribution to the scope and presence of Afro-American literature, Wright did more to advance the cause of blackness than the Communist Party ever did, and the same is true of Baraka. There is nothing original in his present political commitment; all the positions he has held in the course of his career have been held before in Afro-American history. What is original and vital is his artistry. Chairman Baraka simply can't cut it, compared with LeRoi Jones/Amiri Baraka as tale-teller, as black word magician, as, in essence, one of the blues people.

Baudelaire's insight, quoted by Roger Shattuck in *The Innocent Eye: On Modern Literature and the Arts*, has an uncanny relevance to Jones/Baraka's career. The French poet came to the realization that "a system is a kind of damnation which forces us into a perpetual recantation." Always, there is a new conversion, and in order to escape from this "horror," Baudelaire sought refuge in "feeling" (424). It is precisely feeling that energized Baraka's most moving works, even when they manifested the (perhaps necessary) excesses of nationalism and counterracism. The process of definition (or redefinition) that engaged black people, especially in the 1960s, was too intense, too much an outburst of what Reed has termed Jes Grew to be contained in any prescription. Negritude, if we accept that term, is a state of being, not an ideology; with M–L–M, it is just the reverse. Black-ness, not black-ism, is what we are dealing

Figure 6
Revolutionary Dialectics

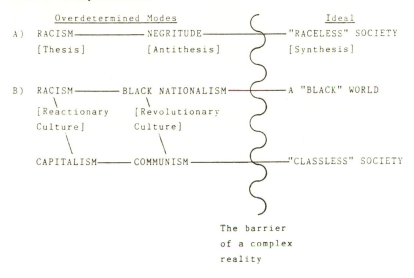

```
        Overdetermined Modes                          Ideal
A)  RACISM———————————— NEGRITUDE—————————————"RACELESS" SOCIETY
    [Thesis]              [Antithesis]              [Synthesis]


B)  RACISM———————— BLACK NATIONALISM————————A "BLACK" WORLD
        \                    \
    [Reactionary         [Revolutionary
    Culture]             Culture]
         \                    \
    CAPITALISM———————— COMMUNISM————————————"CLASSLESS" SOCIETY
```

```
                         The barrier
                         of a complex
                         reality
```

A) is the vision of the black Francophone intellectuals in the African pre-independence era, as codified by Sartre in Black Orpheus.

B) is the dual-stage vision of Jones/Baraka.

with: creative continuity, changing sameness, not the ready-mades of materialist "science."[9]

Throughout his various postures and periods, Jones/Baraka has at least been consistent in his antibourgeois attitude. From beatnik to black nationalist, from Mau-Mau to Mao, he always has striven for an avant-garde, antagonistic position from which to harry the middleclass from which he fled.[10] Furthermore, Baraka has been willing to subject his life and opinions to rigorous self-scrutiny and self-criticism. His fiction is a preeminent example of this, constituting a ruthless display of the author's own flayed image, the cast-off skin of a former, emphatically rejected being. Recently, too, Baraka has apologized for his anti-Semitic and homophobic pro-

nouncements, and he likewise has revised his position on women—
from a defense of inequality based on notions of Africanity to a
rejection of "anti-woman ideology" (*Confirmation: An Anthology of
African American Women*, 17).

It is not Baraka's protean progression that is troubling, for it is
an aspect of his own changing sameness, as well as a very American
desire to always be on the cutting edge of experience. There are
more blatant examples: consider, for one, Jerry Rubin's transformation from Yippie to Yuppie networker and venture-capital camp
follower, which he has justified by claiming, in effect, that capital
is the real avant-garde.[11] Baraka, on the contrary, has remained
steadfastly outside the system, but it is the system which has determined the dynamics of his metamorphosis, for the elasticity and
assimilative powers of late capitalism are such that no single position
of resistance can long remain tenable. The problem with Baraka's
1974 shift from cultural nationalism to M–L–M is that it was a case
of (to use an African expression) "one step forward, two steps
back." The positive aspect lies in Baraka's abandonment of a di-
chotomized racial perspective with a specifically American base and
an advance to an internationalist position that puts First World
complexities and contradictions into a context that embraces Third
World problematics as well and draws a necessary link between the
two. As the ideological papers of the Congress of Afrikan People
(of which Baraka was a leading member) demonstrate, his change
of viewpoint resulted from the influence of the pan-Africanism and
socialist theory of Nkrumah, Amilcar Cabral, and others, as well
as his violent disillusionment with the performance of black officials
whom he had helped get elected in Newark (Sollors, 225). One can
readily understand the initial seductiveness—for an individual such
as Baraka, so committed to black causes—of the revolutionary potential of the newly independent African states, but the sad fact is
that socialism, of either the "African" or more orthodox Euro-
Asian variety, thus far has been a total failure wherever it has been
instituted on the African continent. The other side of the coin, it
must be said, is that capitalism, too, has been a disaster, the apparent
"successes" of Kenya, the Ivory Coast, and so on notwithstanding.
Capitalism merely has exacerbated and exploited, through the more
subtle stranglehold of neo-colonialism, the structural vagaries
wrought by an earlier imperialism. This puts Africa in the tragic

situation of being trapped between two "inherited" but inappropriate alternatives and, simultaneously, of being too dependent economically and technologically to freely evolve, or endeavor to create, indigenous routes into the future. Hence, when Reed, in *The Terrible Twos*, has Nigeria and Uganda ready to confront the United States as presumptive equals by 1990, we are being offered a pan-African dream that, as the processes of negative development continue unabated, daily becomes more utopian, if not downright fantastic.

Notes

The System of Dante's Hell

1. This is suggestive of what one might call the "violence of rebirth" in many Afro-American novels: among them, Wright's *Native Son*, Ellison's *Invisible Man*, and Jones's *System*. Indeed, there are many intriguing similarities in the symbolism of the three authors. One example is the womb image conjoining the theme of rebirth. There is a direct link between the subterranean world of Wright's tale "The Man Who Lived Underground," the "burrow" of Invisible Man (a.k.a. Jack-the-Bear), and the cave of the phantasmagorical wake at the end of *System*.

2. In Delany's *Tales of Nevèrÿon*, a feminist genesis attributes the loss of paradise to a failure to maintain harmony.

3. According to Dante's schema, the deepest part of hell is reserved for those who betray their masters and patrons. However, this is the theology of the privileged, not of the oppressed, which is why Jones puts "heretics" (betrayers of their people, of themselves) at the very bottom.

Tales

4. Richard Wright's Bigger Thomas wishes he could become a pilot and "fly"—escape the gravity of oppression that keeps him and others like him on those mean streets. LeRoi Jones actually joins the air force, only to discover that it is just another "error farce" (*Autobiography*, 94).

5. Sun Ra also has a prominent place in an African short story very similar to "Answers in Progress," in which Earth is conquered by extraterrestrials whom the Africans "assimilate" through the combined influence of jazz and palm wine. (See Emmanuel Boundzéki Dongala, "Jazz and Palm Wine," in the anthology of the same title edited by Willfried F. Feuser [London: Longman, 1981], 194–202.)

6. What Baraka calls "the defense of my psyche" (*Autobiography*, 38) has a great deal to do with his intellectual/creative strategies for leadership and vanguard roles, his shifting/evolving stances of image and ideology. The fiction is of particular importance because it examines this motivational complex, as Baraka himself suggests when he confesses that in writing *System*, "I consciously wrote as deep into my psyche as I could go," and that it was like a descent into hell (*Autobiography*, 166)—the hell of self-confrontation, of self-revulsion, later followed by a rebirth of consciousness.

7. If *Invisible Man* is referred to frequently in this study, if it is deconstructed by Jones in *System* and parodied by Reed in *The Freelance Pallbearers*, it is because Ralph Ellison's novel exists as the summa of Afro-American literary modernism, the text against which subsequent writers have had to measure themselves. (Reed's *The Last Days of Louisiana Red* is also a partial parody of Richard Wright's *Native Son*, another of the principal canonical texts in modern Afro-American writing.) *Invisible Man* occupies in black American letters a position similar to the one *Ulysses* occupies in English literature—a culmination, a creative summation of all that went before, but with this difference: whereas Joyce adopts his organizing structure from classical antiquity, enfolding the deficiencies of the present in the myth-rich contours of the Greek past from which Western civilization traces its origins, Ellison's protagonist reenacts an odyssey symbolizing the travels and travails of a displaced people, testimonialized in black autobiography, beginning with the earliest slave narratives. In *Invisible Man*, the black American experience turns back on itself to see its fullness wholly articulated for the first time.

... & After

8. Perhaps the argument with regard to which is the "authentic" tradition in Afro-American literature, the "revolutionary" or the "assimilative," can be partially resolved by linking them through the re/visionary aspect they both share.

9. Louisa Teish refers to capitalism, communism, chauvinism, racism, and such, as the "*Ism* Brothers" (144). Baraka habitually has hung out with some of these "brothers"; Delany never has. Reed does seem to have the monkey of sexism on his back, but it is, for all that, a *signifyin'* monkey.

10. Baraka always has been ashamed of, and reacted against, his middleclass origins; Reed is defiantly proud of his; Delany simply views it as having been an advantage. Black art, in the final analysis, always may have drawn its sustenance from below, from the core of black life, but the fact is that a good deal of Afro-American literature is, and has been, written by people who are (in quotation marks, if you will) "bourgeois."

11. Cf. Hal Foster: "The real radicality is always capital's, for it not only effects the new symbolic forms by which we live but also destroys the old. More than any avant-garde, capital is the agent of transgression and shock" (147).

3

Ishmael Reed

GATHERING THE LIMBS OF OSIRIS

The Freelance Pallbearers

While LeRoi Jones's autobiographical fictions are often grammatically disjunctive, deadly serious, and essentially "realistic," Reed's first novel, which contains some (drastically transposed) autobiographical elements, is, contrastingly, satirical and surrealistic. It is not a personal exorcism, like Jones's *System*, but a national exorcism, an art-if-act similar to the Yippie "attempt" to levitate the Pentagon by means of an incantatory "reading." Reed prefers a "writing" (with its associative connotations of "rite-ing" and "righting"), a scriptural "mumbo jumbo" which, like the traditional African masquerade, combines profundity with hilarity.

Bukka Doopeyduk, narrator of *Pallbearers*, is an incredibly naive, bumbling character reminiscent of the protagonist of Nathanael West's *A Cool Million* (1934), a work which is not only a brilliant, bitter parody of Horatio-Alger but a parody of Christianity as well (the Nazarene Creed of *Pallbearers*). The gradual destruction of Bukka's illusions and his final crucifixion parallel the literal dismantlement of West's antihero.

Bukka is a "brainwashed Negro . . . who believes in everything that SAM runs down" (9) and who is similarly tranquilized by the Nazarene Creed, which has instilled him with an excessive humility and passivity. Keith Byerman reminds us that Bukka means "Booker/Book" (220), suggesting that one of the "sources" being parodied is Booker T. Washington's *Up from Slavery*. Bukka's problem is that he has been (mis)shaped by a study of, and allegiance to, the wrong text(s). (The "antiseptic boplicity" that Bukka defends suggests the white washing or neutralizing of countercultural forms of expression, a strategy of making the word "safe" for the system to absorb, that Reed explores in greater detail in his subsequent works. The Wallflower Order's desperate search for an antidote to Jes Grew in *Mumbo Jumbo* is the paradigmatic example.) He is so content with his condition—indeed, it is only after many disorienting experiences that he even becomes aware of the negative aspects of his situation in SAM—that he is overjoyed to be awarded a golden bedpan. A voodoo adept is awarded the *asson* as a recognition of his powers; Bukka, not a *houngan* by any stretch of the imagination, receives this parody of the *asson* as a symbol of his ineffectuality. However, to escape being duped by words is not as simple as changing language, a fact that is brought home at the very end of the novel, when the *capital*-ized message, though written in Chinese, remains the same. The language has changed but not the text, which can only change when there is a corresponding change of reality, of consciousness.

On at least one level, *Pallbearers* is an extended parody of *Invisible Man*. It is impractical and unnecessary to catalogue all the possible examples, but a few will suffice to make my point. The advice of Sam's mother to her son on her deathbed parodies the advice given to Invisible Man's family by his dying grandfather; Invisible Man's expulsion from college is paralleled by Bukka's resignation; Bukka's "crying-the-blues" recalls Trueblood; his job emptying bedpans parallels Invisible Man's job in the factory basement; Hairyman's recruitment of Bukka on the basis of his speech is a counterpart to Brother Jack's recruitment of Invisible Man into the Brotherhood; I am even tempted to hear linguistic echoes of Ellison's opening sentence, "I am an invisible man," in Reed's opener, "I live in HARRY SAM."

To give another, more general, instance, Bukka, who "normally" fawns and shuffles, becomes aggressive when he is hoodooed by his in-laws, who are in cahoots with Sam. However, his aggression is atavistic; he is turned into a Hollywood-style werewolf. Eventually, he is de-hoodooed, but he becomes aggressive again in a more positive sense when he realizes that he has been a dupe, a kind of zombie—in other words, he always has been hoodooed, hoodwinked, under the spell of Sam and the Nazarene

Creed. Ellison's Invisible Man not only "discovers" his own invisibility, he has to learn, finally, to see through the invisibility of the true sources of his oppression, which involves a progressive "unmasking" of reality (that same masquerading mode that Rinehart has turned to his own advantage). Bukka goes through the same process, albeit in a parodic context. *Pallbearers*, indeed, is a kind of minstrel version of *Invisible Man*.

Geoffrey Hartman has reminded us of Valery's forecast of the danger that modern European culture might end up "as an 'infinitely rich nothing' " (xv–xvi). The truth of such a danger can be ascertained in late twentieth-century America, with its high-tech ambience and upwardly mobile hollow men. Reed's multiethnic cultural campaign, a re/visionary and resurrectional enterprise, addresses itself directly to this dilution and debasement of the rounded fullness of life. His writings and organizational activities also constitute acts of disobedience to the authority of canonical tradition, which essentially has been restrictive and elitist.

It is worth noting, however, that something like a canonical tradition has operated within black culture itself, where the values of the black bourgeoisie enthroned certain "refined" forms at the expense of those perceived as threats to their status as potential *assimilados* in a white-dominated world. The black minstrel shows, for example, were ignored by the nineteenth-century black press (which spoke to and for the black bourgeoisie), for it was mainly the black masses who attended these performances. The blues, too, was a rural and working-class phenomenon disparaged by the bourgeoisie, but rejection came from another trajectory as well.

From the outright anti-black-cultural chauvinism of the . . . American Communist Party, to the contradictory "nationalism" of such all-black organizations as Marcus Garvey's United Negro Improvement Association or Cyril Briggs's African Blood Brotherhood, the blues and jazz were ignored if not actually condemned. (Garon, 65)

It might be argued (it has been said of the blues as well) that the black minstrels presented an exaggerated or stereotypical view of black reality—but in whose eyes? "Unlike whites, [blacks] *knew* the diversity of black people. . . . They laughed at the familiar in exaggerated form. At least in part, theirs was in-group laughter of recognition, even of belonging" (Toll, 258). The crucial word is diversity. The *embourgeoisment* of black American culture is a danger that makes cultural nationalism a still-significant posture, as I have already argued, for as John Langston Gwaltney notes, core black culture, whose values he defines as being "rooted in a lengthy peasant tradition and clandestine theology," "*is* the mainstream" for the black American masses (xxvi, xxiii). This suggests, too, the inappropriateness of reductionist ideologies like Marxism–Leninism–Mao Tse-tung Thought, with their culture-destroying imperatives.

HARRY SAM is Uncle Sam—America—as well as a cartoon version of various U.S. presidents. It also brings to mind "Sam's plantation," an expression used by a minstrel of the Civil War period to describe the Union (Toll, 108). SAM, however, is identifiable with more than simply the nation or its chief of state; it is a mode of consciousness, characterized by a desire for mastery and control. HARRY SAM, then, could be read as "Harass 'em," a statement of the sort of belligerence toward "outsiders" that our foreign policy (and often our domestic policy) has manifested. Indeed, if Reed's first novel is, at its crudest level, a dramatization of the colloquialism "the shit hits the fan," it is not only because of an internal uproar in the bowels of SAM but also because of drastic dis-ease in the rest of the world. The overseas Yam insurgencies, for example, may be a punning reference to the war of Vietnam, which U.S. soldiers called 'Nam, but they are a specific allusion to African unrest and probably, too, an oblique allusion to the yam-eating scene in *Invisible Man*, where the yam, soul food, becomes the manna of a reinformed consciousness for the narrator. In any case, as the bulletins from Radio UH-O (a yellow back radio?) and the Chinese "conquest" of HARRY SAM suggest, the Third World cannot be ignored—a point driven home again by the influence of Haiti on the hoodooing of America in *Mumbo Jumbo* and the rise of African nations to world-power status in *The Terrible Twos*.

The creation and manipulation of desire which underlies our acquisitive, consumption-mad society is symbolized in *Pallbearers* by the frequent litany EATS EATS EATS—an American mantra that is both a noun and a verb, suggesting the omnivorousness of our sur/reality. Even the Nazarene apocalypse, with its bars of soap and champagne bubbles, reflects the "gospel" of advertising. However, as the ever-present image of the commode—Sam's "throne"—reminds us, the end-product of all this consumption is shit. Sam is a coprocrat, presiding over a literal waste/land of defecation and death. (There is an interesting etymological link between commode, which in its adjectival form means convenient, and commodity, which has the archaic meaning of convenience. Indeed, a euphemism for commode is "convenience.") Both the act of buying and the act of evacuating are pleasurable, but compulsive concern with the latter can lead to perversion; Reed is suggesting that the same is true of compulsive greed.

The excremental vision in *Pallbearers* is, among other things, a comment on the state of the environment, involving both literal and spiritual pollution. The action of Dean Polyglot, who pretends to be a dung beetle in order to experience Gregor Samsa's metamorphosis, is a significant example. Figuratively speaking, the dean, like most of the inhabitants of HARRY SAM, is an insect pushing excrement. By the end of the novel, this excrement dwarfs the landscape. The endeavor to achieve "relevance" and authenticity, ridiculous in this instance in the first place, has become Sisyphean, and the country's waste products have literally become a threat to its existence. It is interesting to note that in ancient Egyptian, *kheper*, the word for scarab or dung beetle, designates not only the insect and its symbolic metamorphoses but also refers to *becoming* (Lamy, 14). The question is, what are we becoming, what have we already become?

A further connection can be established between the Egyptian concept of the *ka*, the double of the soul (*ba*), and the dung beetle, via the following pun/association: ka-ka (a doubling) = caca = shit. This is not only a suggestion of spiritual pollution; on a less pejorative level it is a reminder that matter and spirit are inextricable and associated, respectively, with the alchemy of the body and the alchemy of the mind. Freud, Norman O. Brown, Egyptian religion, scatological satire all provide the bases for different readings of Reed's imagery in *Pallbearers*, and the density of allusion, the deliberate levels of meaning—zany and frivolous only on the surface—derive from what one might term a psychoarchaeological investigation of a rich, riotous period in American history, the 1960s. Jones, in *System*, wants to jam our faces in his shit, he tells us, as a deliberate assault on our ignorance and aloofness; Reed wants to jam America's face in its own collective shit in order to read there, perhaps, its current state of health, ill or otherwise.

The Freelance Pallbearers themselves remind one of the biblical admonition, "Let the dead bury their dead." Their name could be that of a contemporary rock group, but Reed intends something more serious here. The implication, again, is that this is a world full of dead or dying things, of waste—products of a too-rampant materialism—yet even the "burial" of this refuse can only be had for a price. The Freelance Pallbearers, in a sense, are entrepreneurs of the end.

Yellow Back Radio Broke-Down

If *Pallbearers*, with its hallucinatory pop imagery and hoodooistic "boplicity," heralded a nearly unprecedented voice in American literature, *Yellow Back Radio Broke-Down*, Reed's second novel, is no less auspicious. The titles of both books are bizarre, cryptic encodings (which, however, the works make "sense" of as they unfold), while Reed's language remains supercharged, idiosyncratic, traditional, side-splitting and surreal all at the same time: "Folks. This here is the story of the Loop Garoo Kid. A cowboy so bad he made a working posse of spells phone in sick. . . . A desperado so onery he made the Pope cry and the most powerful of cattlemen shed his head to the Executioner's swine" (9). The tone of this speech is preeminently American. (It is the language of the West in more ways than one.) This is the colloquial narrative style of the tall tale, an oral form of literature; it is the granddaddy of radio soap opera, an aural form, and the ancestor, as well, of the visual mythifications of television and cinema.

The time is ostensibly the nineteenth century, but it is, as is often the case with Reed's fiction, more properly a segment of time set adrift like an immense iceberg in the ocean of history (which includes the present and the future as well as the past). Encased in this "ice," reflected through many facets as in a well-cut gem, is a critical moment, a bit of psychic germ-plasm, of broad significance to the American character. Reed's strategy is to isolate and dramatize this particular nexus, and then to bring it into contact with other mythohistorical confluences, allowing them to resonate together with resultant vibrations that should "tune in" the reader.

Yellow Back Radio, after all, can be "adjusted" to the correct frequency (22). Control of the media can enable one to dominate people's thoughts, but control of history enables one to manipulate people's psyches, their very sense of who and what they are.

The emanations from Yellow Back Radio constitute the tribal noise of Western civilization, the dissonant frequencies of an exploded symphony (sin-phony), bad news broadcast from the bowels of an unhealthy giant. The rooftops of Yellow Back, appearing like "blue tubes" in a storm, are a reminder that this particular locale is broadcasting trouble, but they also may symbolize the fact that Yellow Back Radio is a station capable of transmitting the "intricate rhythms" and "spaced out sounds" produced by the Native Americans and blacks who have influenced American society profoundly, despite the best efforts of the Drag Gibsons and their ilk. Therefore, it is pleasant to imagine that when Yellow Back Radio's signals grow faint, it is because of a melt-down due to the power of the "blues."

The Loop Garoo Kid is Lucifer, bringer of light, the rebel angel, Satan. He is also Prometheus, who comes to Earth to free mankind from the tyranny of the gods. (Satan, tempting Eve and Adam to eat from the Tree of Knowledge, performs precisely the same function.) The idea of angels descending from heaven and passing themselves off as human is referred to in black folklore as "mangelizing." Reed has "mangelized" the personae of Judeo-Christian divinity. The struggles in heaven, one could say, are rather bluntly brought down to earth.

A loup garou is, literally, a werewolf, a creature of metamorphosis. Reed anglicized the term into Loop Garoo, and it is significant that the truncated vowel *u* has been replaced by the continuous, containing vowel *o*, the omphalos or mystic naught. (This may have been on the analogy of *voudou—voodoo*.) A loop is itself continuous, and the Loop Garoo Kid straddles time: from ancient Egypt to modern Las Vegas and beyond. Loop also suggests the completion of an electrical circuit, which is fitting in the context of the radio/video imagery the novel exploits, and which reappears in *Mumbo Jumbo* in the reference to the "electric" loa with the Yellow Back. Furthermore, to "knock for a loop is to throw into confusion. . . . Once you get to the multiple meanings, you, the reader, begin to loop" (Nazareth, 219).

The Kid is not only a black cowboy with a cleft foot—a cowboy version of High John the Conqueror, the superhero of slave folklore—he was also born with ghost lobes and a caul over his face: the signs of a "two-head" or hoodoo man (indeed, Loop is a founder of the American Hoodoo Church). "Two-head" actually means having two minds, which is beautifully apt, given the fact that Loop is in the forefront of the conflict between those who view reality in more than one sense and those who insist that there is only one sense.

Loop claims that he is engaged in the creation of a "horse opera," which is what *Yellow Back Radio* is on two different levels. First, there is the traditional sense of a "western," that immensely popular genre of both fiction and film. However, there is also another important meaning, for a "horse" is one who becomes possessed (ridden) by a deity, so that what we really have is a *hoodoo* western.[1]

The Pope, Loop's principal adversary in the novel, is referred to as Innocent but is not otherwise directly identified. Several popes took that name, and the nearest hint we have to this one's specific identity is Loop's mention of the Inquisition. The Inquisition, both as fact and as metaphor, is significant in terms of the novel's thematic structure and Reed's concerns in general (an inquiry into the truths of experience that have been neglected or condemned by the forces of intolerance, and an antidotal "fixing" of the inquisitional, persecutional tendencies of the powerful and privileged). Elsewhere, Reed has identified the Pope as Innocent VIII, whose reign, interestingly enough, ended in the year of Columbus's voyage to America.[2] The significance of Innocent VIII, however, is in fact his issuance in 1484 of a papal bull deploring the spread of witchcraft and authorizing two inquisitors to investigate and extirpate it. They published their findings two years later in the famous *Malleus Maleficarum*, or Witches' Hammer (mentioned in the novel [162]), and ironically came under suspicion of heresy themselves because of the forbidden knowledge they had gained (O'Keefe, 526). That knowledge is power and can be a kind of contagion is one of Reed's central motifs. One might say that the Loop Garoo Kid takes the papal bull by the horns, for Hoodoo has some statements of its own to make. Keith Thomas, in his impressive study *Religion and the Decline of Magic*, has amply documented the way in which officially sanctioned creeds forced unofficial beliefs underground, but the fact is, "magic as a planetary heritage is never lost and easily revives under stress" (O'Keefe, 506).

In a sense, however, it is unnecessary to "pin down" the Pope by number; it is the symbolic as well as historical qualities of his role which are of primary significance, in addition to his name— Innocent—an example, here, of cosmic irony. Reed has taken the Pope out of his specifically Catholic context and transferred him to a place in myth. Innocent is actually Loop's alter ego. They are intimates who need each other. They exist side by side like the two elements of the symbolic device Reed employs in this novel— ● ◯ —which I have commented upon in some detail elsewhere.[3] As in magnetism, opposites attract, like poles repel. Loop, "cheated out of his martyrdom" at the last minute, takes off in pursuit of the Pope, who is heading back to his "point of origin," the realm of archetypes. Now that they have acted out their respective roles, they can return to their natural camaraderie, freed from the necessity of taking themselves seriously.

Yellow Back Radio is like a region of the Inferno—not Dante's, this time, but that particularly American hell that President Dean Clift visits in *The Terrible Twos*. This hell—an Expressionist vision of repressed desires run amuck—provides the antipodes to the leg- endary American paradise sought by conquistadors and immigrants alike. One of the obvious things Reed is trying to demonstrate via the surrealism of his fictions is that the American Dream has more often than not proved to be an American Nightmare, especially for minorities. The idea is to turn the nightmare back on those whose "sleep of reason" has caused so much trouble for everyone else. So, *"This time the witches win"* (43). The Saxon word *wych* means to turn or bend. This lends significant resonance to Reed's intro- duction of a new loa through a dance called "The Our Turn" (*Conjure*, 83). If witches—hoodoos—are benders of reality, en- deavoring to turn things back in the direction of multiplicity rather than monopoly, of toleration rather than repression, it is because of the imbalance wrought by the relentless aggression and alienation of the Atonist dispensation Reed addresses most particularly in *Mumbo Jumbo*. This suggests another dimension to "turn," which, in Afro-American usage, refers to traditional civility, the demon- strative evidence of having been raised properly (Gwaltney, xvii). The fragmenting of a holistic vision of reality, the assaults upon

Nature that "civilization" has mounted, reveal a serious lack of respect for the "propers" of a balanced existence.

One of the crucial encounters in *Yellow Back Radio* is that between the Loop Garoo Kid as "outlaw" artist and Bo Shmo, the social realist vigilante. The two sides of this debate, roughly corresponding to the ideological warfare between "committed" and "individualist" forces during the Black Arts movement, remains relevant even now, twenty years later, though the emphases have shifted somewhat, with results that are ironically implicating for some of the combatants, as I shall have reason to suggest later on.

Bo Shmo's position is essentially the one promulgated in LeRoi Jones's famous poem "Black Art," as Bo's claim that a landscape is only valuable if it depicts the oppressor hanging from a tree reveals. Loop (and Reed) cannot tolerate these prescriptive demands, which amount to straitjacketing the imagination in the name of "revolutionary" necessity. Bo's description of Loop's work as "a blur and a doodle" is intended as a put-down, but the blur and the doodle can be read; they are signs for those who can recognize them. What matter if there is no ideological "clarity"? After all, for most black artists, form follows Funk.[4]

Reed's novels bear the same relationship to more formalistic black fiction that the black storefront churches have with regard to the larger, more middleclass black churches—they are informal, improvisational, spontaneous, syncretic. Reed's writings even may be linked to the time-honored tradition of pamphleteering, for a pamphlet can be as diverse in form or content as the imaginative or polemical demands of its author require. Loop Garoo's rejoinder to Bo Shmo, insisting on the novel's freedom, its protean qualities, could also serve as a fitting description of the polymorphous nature of pamphlets.

In the language of the Old West, "riding sign" meant to ride the range in search of cattle that had either been stolen or had strayed. The Loop Garoo Kid, as black cowboy and voodoo *vaquero*, and Reed, as "pagan" metaphysician, are riding sign themselves in the sense of following and rounding up lost or stolen meanings of a cultural past that has been assaulted, vilified, and obscured. Similarly, although the junction near Yellow Back Radio is named Video, it inevitably suggests, in this western context, the word it replaces, *rodeo*, which originally meant to round up or encircle, thus connecting it with the idea of riding sign. Rodeo later came to mean a contest of skills—precisely what we have between Loop and his adversaries—and later still a form of entertainment, which is one thing a novel can be, among other possibilities, as Loop insists and Reed demonstrates.

The "contest of wits" that takes place during Carnival "when one Speech Band encounters another" on the Caribbean island of Tobago (Abrahams, 7) strikes me as another useful metaphor for the "contest" between diverse black artists, each representing different registers of the black aesthetic continuum. It is perfectly analogous to the way in which each jazz soloist pushes his colleagues to greater heights of invention upon, and extension of, collectively stated themes. In fact, just as Carnival "explores the realms of aesthetic transport involved in sudden freedom from restraints" (Abrahams, 103), so, too, black music and black literature explore the transcendency that aesthetic freedom can evoke. Jes Grew, the spiritual nexus of Neo-Hoodoo, which we discuss in the next chapter, is the carnival impulse personified.

It is for this reason that I believe Terry Castle's discussion of the carnivalization of eighteenth-century narrative is apropos for our examination of Reed, especially if one considers the role of Carnival in black culture. Bakhtin's suggestion, which Castle refers to, that "the carnivalized work . . . resists generic classification and instead combines . . . a multiplicity of literary modes in a single increasingly 'promiscuous' form" (912), is certainly applicable to works like *Mumbo Jumbo*. Further, Castle's description of carnival (or masquerade) as associated with "patterns of ideological destabilization" (910), with "institutionalized dreams of disorder" (912) dramatizing possibilities of change and functioning culturally as a "discontinuous, estranging, sometimes even hallucinatory event that nonetheless carrie[s] with it a powerfully cathartic and disruptive cognitive éclat" (913) applies to both jazz and Jes Grew; it is, in fact, the operative mode of Neo-Hoodooism.[5]

Mumbo Jumbo

Reed's third novel, *Mumbo Jumbo* (1972), probably his best-known work, is his supreme achievement to date, on its own amply justifying Fredric Jameson's estimation of Reed as one of the principal postmodern artists (118).

Mumbo Jumbo is an historico-aesthetic textbook, complete with illustrations, bibliography, and footnotes. It is Reed's dissertation on the metaphysics of consciousness and, simultaneously, a filmscript: though taking place primarily in New York, it opens with a prologue in New Orleans, following which Reed "rolls" the title and credits before plunging back into the story. The cinematic aspect is played up from the beginning: the first reference to Jes Grew as "a Creeping Thing" immediately brings to mind a Hollywood horror film, and the people dancing on hospital carts while the doctor is "slipping dipping gliding" is like a Marx Brothers comedy (3, 6). (In fact, monster movies, slapstick, and detective films—*Mumbo Jumbo*, after all, is a "mystery"—all are significant influences on Reed's fiction which await more detailed analysis.)

The "heterophany of elements" found in Reed's work, which *Mumbo Jumbo* exploits with particular brilliance, derives not only from modernist collage and postmodernist bricolage techniques, it is found as well in jazz (Jahn, 99), which, it is important to recognize, was the first mode of both black American modernism and postmodernism. This "heterophany of elements" is also a feature of Jes Grew and is analogous to the syncretization of the worship of African and other deities in Voodoo, the many varieties of gumbo, and such, which are found in Afro-American experience. Impromptu variations, based on individual refinement of collective knowledge, are crucial. There is a common saying among Yoruba masqueraders: Kò síbi tá ì í gbé dáná alẹ̀ / Ọbẹ̀ ní ó dùn ju'ra wọn lo (There is no house where supper is not prepared/But one stew tastes better than another). This is a form of artistic criticism used to distinguish one oral performer from another in terms of excellence, employing the same idea of recipe as Reed's poem "The Neo-Hoodoo Aesthetic" (*Conjure*, 26), where everything depends upon the "cook."[6]

However, the polyglot quality of *Mumbo Jumbo* may have another source: the slave narratives. Citing their "extremely mixed nature," James Olney offers the following description of what might be included:

an engraved portrait or photograph of the subject of the narrative; authenticating testimonials, prefixed or postfixed; poetic epigraphs, snatches of poetry in the text, poems appended; illustrations . . . ; interruptions of the narrative by way of declamatory addresses to the reader . . . ; a bewildering variety of documents—letters to and from the narrator, bills of sale, newspaper clippings, notices of slave auctions and of escaped slaves . . . ; and sermons and anti-slavery speeches and essays tacked on at the end to demonstrate the post-narrative activities of the narrative (49).

Many of these elements are to be found in *Mumbo Jumbo* and in *Flight to Canada* (Reed's fifth novel, a deliberate parody of slave narratives). It is further proof of the correctness of Reed's position when he denies that his work is derived from white models. Black literature and black art have their own lineage, their own heritage of experimentation and innovation. The uprooted (Africans in the Diaspora) have proven to be masters of rootwork, and, indeed, the concern with roots is a form of spiritual ecology, the preservation of the signs and symbols of a culture.

Art, for Reed, is life. This is one of the reasons he personifies art "objects" in his short fiction "Cab Calloway Stands In for the Moon." Rin Tin Rover's "escaped" treasures have been, in a sense, enslaved: torn from their proper cultural context, placed in the "service" of the privileged conquistador/colonizer. They are valuable not in the spiritual terms of value they embodied for their creators and the societies where they were originally situated, but in terms now of money; they represent investments. Slaveowners looked upon their slave "possessions" in the same way. (A principal reason Massa Swille, in *Flight to Canada*, wants his runaway slave Quickskill back is that he paid good money for him.)

In "Cab Calloway," art escapes from confinement to rejoin life; in *Mumbo Jumbo*, art is liberated through the efforts of an international, multiethnic organization called the *Mu'tafikah*,[7] whose efforts to liberate and restore stolen artifacts not only parallels Isis's labors in collecting the scattered pieces of Osiris's dismembered body but also provides a metaphor for Reed's own attempts to render a true black aesthetic by rescuing it from co-option, misunderstanding, and dogmatism.

Mumbo Jumbo is a novel about the Jazz Age, which is also the Age of Prohibition, with all that that implies. At the beginning of that crucial decade of the 1920s, revolutionary saxophonist Charlie "Yardbird" Parker is born and Warren G. Harding is president.

Bird is a quintessential representative of the Jes Grew impulse, a supreme practitioner. Harding was inept and his administration extremely corrupt. Ironically, Harding declared a "return to normalcy" as the government's policy; in other words, "the business" as usual. However, Reed is at some pains to show that there is some heavy if inconclusive competition from another, older Business: the firm of Jes Grew & Company.

Indeed, the manner in which Reed plays with terms like "business" and "work" is suggestive of the way in which his writing displaces ideas from clichéd or conventional contexts and lends them a different, "redemptive" significance. For example, "The Work" is not a literary artifact; it is, rather, an ongoing process. "The Ndembu call what a ritual specialist does, *kuzata*, 'work' " (Turner, 30). This is the sort of "work" Reed is referring to; it has magical rather than Marxist/capitalist meaning. For Reed, there is a definite distinction between "workers" and "Workers" (see *The Last Days of Louisiana Red*, 6–8). Similarly, Ed Yellings's Solid Gumbo Works is, as a Business, more discorporate than incorporated, part of that form of Free Enterprise that equals Art/Work.

Jes Grew creates the Jazz Age in two important ways. First, it is the source of all that is vital and vibrant. While some diseases cause the body to waste away, Jes Grew enlivens the host. It causes people to groove, bang, and jive around instead of acting like candidates for the Wallflower Order. It is the presiding spirit of the Saturday Night Function, which, in Albert Murray's characterization, reads like a working definition of Neo-Hoodoo: "in addition to its concern with forthright confrontation and expurgation, [it] also consists of rituals of resilience and perseverance through improvisation in the face of capricious disjuncture." Furthermore, the "primary emphasis is placed upon aesthetics not ethics" (42). Jes Grew's second important role in creating the Jazz Age is its illumination of the contradictions inherent in American society and, by extension, Western civilization in general. For as Jes Grew spreads, liberating masses of people from their psychological shackles (causing them to "desert their masters," white or black), the forces of repression and intolerance are increasingly pressed into showing their Hand. Jes Grew literally threatens the end of civilization insofar as it is a mode of existence that is restrictive, violent, and unnatural.

Reed's conspiracy theory of history posits a secret society known as the Atonist Path, protected by a militant organization called the Wallflower Order. Atonist means follower of Aton, the One God that Akhenaton (Amenhotep IV, 1379–1372 B.C.) imposed upon his pantheistic subjects, who, after his death, immediately reverted to their traditional beliefs, even abandoning the new city built by the pharaoh as a center for Atonist worship. (This provides Reed with an historical precedent for his desire to bring back the old cults and abandon the "new" dispensation with its exclusivist tendencies.) An Atonist is also "one who atones"—a Judeo-Christian. The Jews, and then the Christians and Moslems after them, were able to consolidate the abortive gains that Akhenaton had made on behalf of monotheism, with the result that alternative forms of belief were systematically suppressed. Thus, according to Reed, Moses is one of the principal villains in the Voodoo tradition because he "stole" its secrets from Jethro.[8] Unfortunately, Moses was invested with the Petro ("hot") *asson* instead of the Rada ("sweet"); in other words, he was a follower of the Left Hand Path rather than the Right Hand.

The Left Hand Path is described in Reed's self-designated most experimental writing, "Cab Calloway Stands In for the Moon." It is comparable to the Atonist Path and clearly represents a negative, destructive force. There is an Akan proverb that only a fool points to his origins with his left hand. In Yoruba, the ọwọ́ àlàáfíá (hand of peace) is used as a euphemism for ọwọ́ òsì (the left hand) because lefthandedness is considered a bad thing, as can be seen in the fact that the word òsì (left) is found in the compound òlòsì, meaning an awful or wretched person. This negative view of leftwardness appears to be deeply rooted in the human psyche. In one psychologist's investigations of people's attitudes, left was regarded as bad, dark, profane, and female, while right was held to be the opposite. Left is often seen as "the area of the taboo, the sacred, the unconscious, the feminine, the intuitive, and the dreamer" (Ornstein, 67, 80). In other words, leftwardness has strong connotations of risk, of undesirability if not of danger.

From a physiological perspective, however, the left hemisphere of the brain is concerned with analytical thinking, logic, and verbal functions, and it is essentially linear in its operations, whereas the right hemisphere "seems specialized for holistic mentation" (Ornstein, 67). It is logic, linearity, and so on, so characteristic of the whole Western enterprise, toward which Reed and other critics of its relentless thrust for total domination of reality have become hostile. The right hemisphere of the brain is the one that would be the locus for Neo-Hoodoo, and it is this half of the brain that controls the left side of the body; hence, one can intuit the hostility leftwardness has incurred, for it represents the irrational, the poetic, the realm of forces not shapeable by the tools held in the right hand of technology.

In view of this, one could say that Reed's Neo-Hoodooist strategy involves the "savaging" of the domesticated mind. This speaks directly to the relevance of the primitive, especially with regard to the role of the artist, who explores the mysteries of reality through the enigma of the self extrapolated in imagination. The artist in this sense is a shaman.

The origin of opposition to all of this can be traced beyond Plato to the figure of Set in Egyptian mythology. Set is the unnatural forefather of the Atonists and the arch villain in Reed's cosmology.[9] According to the tradition which Reed retells, Set treacherously murdered his brother Osiris, dismembered him, and scattered abroad the fourteen pieces of his body. Isis went about Egypt in grief, attempting to gather the limbs of her brother/husband. This action is recreated in the division of the Book of Thoth, the sacred anthology which is Jes Grew's ur-Text, into fourteen sections by Wallflower crusader Hinckle Von Vampton, and the subsequent efforts of Jes Grew to seek its Text. It is also reflected in Reed's own attempts to gather up the scattered fragments of a tradition in order to restore a culture, for the scattering of Osiris's limbs is a clear metaphor for the Diaspora.

The Egyptian myth of the conflict between Osiris and Set is very similar to the Dogon myth of Ogo and Nommo, primal males— each with a female twin—created by the supreme god Amma. Ogo, impatient, burst forth prematurely from the placenta within the cosmic egg, thus disordering the universe. Amma was able to re-impose order by sacrificing Nommo and scattering his dismembered body north, south, east, and west. Thereafter, Amma restored Nommo to wholeness and to life and made him master of the universe.

If we rely on the Dogon tale, then the dispersal of the Text of Jes Grew, like the scattering of Nommo's parts, may be said to provide the basis for a future reassertion of creativity. It is clear that Jes Grew seeking its Text is also a metaphor for the Harlem Renaissance, which was basically a New York phenomenon. A single Text, a single locale: a source easy to pin down and "destroy." However, the Text's carbons (black impressions) are scattered all over the country, thus providing the means for a resurgence of Jes Grew; and it is significant that the second renaissance, the Black Arts movement, was not localized but national, with many centers.

In seeking its Text, Jes Grew is struggling to liber/ate its power (in Latin, *liber* means both "free" and "book"). However, if song, dance, and drum have been the traditional repositories for Jes Grew's "eloquence," would not textualization reduce it, reify it, turn it into an object rather than a process? The answer is no, for the Text of Jes Grew will be it "speaking," enabling it to be "heard" by a culture that has fetishized the book. Reed is suggesting that the "arrival" of Afro-American literature is long overdue. However, like Jones/Baraka, like Delany, Reed goes beyond the concept of "text" as exclusively a print structure. Properly understood, Jes Grew's Text is the "text" of black experience as a whole, while its style is that of black vernacular speech.

The search of Jes Grew for its Text symbolizes the effort of black aesthetics of achieve a long-sought foregrounding after a venerable tradition in the *black*ground of the culture. However, it is not only white crusaders who threaten to make Jes Grew fail to find its Speaking; it is, in fact, the black Muslim Abdul Hamid who burns the Text because he believes it to be "lewd, nasty, decadent" (202), after a "Negro editor" has already rejected it for publication on the grounds that it *"lacked 'soul' and wasn't 'Nation' enough"* (98). Reed is here addressing the same hostile forces he dealt with in *Yellow Back Radio*: the "masters" of the West who want to stamp out "the Black Tide of Mud" they fear will inundate their cherished institutions, and those intolerant elements within the black community itself—self-appointed arbiters of taste who seek conformity either to an assimilative code catering to white values, or to a revolutionary prescription such as that espoused by Bo Shmo. Hinckle Von Vampton worries about what would happen if it was impossible to predict minds, and he offends Nathan Brown with his reference to the "Negro Experience" because Brown feels it is just another way of implying that all black people experience the world in the same way (117). Similarly, Major Young informs Von Vampton that black writers all have unique styles and asks, "Is it necessary for us to write the same way?" (102). However, the black demand for black artists to toe a particular line with regard to envisioning and articulating the reality of blackness amounts to much the same argument. Compare Baraka: "We need a value *system* to be *predictable* in our behavior" (*Kawaida Studies: The New Nationalism*, 12; my emphasis). Again, discussing the third principle of Nguzo Saba (Ujima, collective work and responsibility), Baraka says, "The I's must be our many eyes" (11). However, if the "I's" are the "many eyes" of black collectivity, this must be an implicit acknowledgment of individuality's importance, unless we are to assume that all seeings are the same—which then puts us back in the camp of the Von Vamptons, the ideological mind-set of Set.

Racial differences notwithstanding, all of these tendencies are in agreement in labeling as "unnatural" that which Reed views as natural and whole. The fetish of "discipline" and authoritarianism exhibited by Atonists, the elaborate rituals, secret societies, and powerful "orders" themselves amount to a form of "mumbo jumbo," a term more fitting for the engineering of repression than for the free expression of natural impulses. Jes Grew *is* natural, as its name implies; efforts to combat it, like the Talking Android, are artificial and contrived. It is for this reason that we can see Reed's writings as addressing America, not so much in light of Freud's reputed assessment—"a mistake"—as in keeping with Robert Hayden's description of this country as "a problem in metaphysics" (195). In *Mumbo Jumbo*, what we have is a "mystery war"—not just an imperialist incursion into Haiti that the establishment would like to keep secret, but a war *between* mysteries or between mystery and its absence. It is a conflict between "universalism" (as a camouflage for singularity) and multiplicity; between Pl/atonism and pantheism; between "Do as we do" and Hoodoo.

If the Templars, that elite corps of militants of which Hinckle Von Vampton is Grand Master, are heretics, worshiping the black god Baphomet, why then do they fight on the side of the Atonists? Obviously, they recognize the existence of other forces, other realities, and are willing to employ them to extend their own influence. However, whatever "conversion" may have taken place has occurred on the subconscious level; consciously, they are still in the vanguard of the Aryan camp. The battle against Jes Grew is really an endless holding action, based on repression and exploitation—like slavery, like colonialism and neo-colonialism—of the West against the rest.

Whatever the "lyric" content of Jes Grew, the "tune" is irresistible, and the Wallflower Order is looking for a way to borrow the "jargon" of Jes Grew without being absorbed by it. (Hubert "Safecracker" Gould has managed to make a fortune by ripping off the ideas and expressions of black people and publishing them under his own name.) "You're grooving with the jive, H.," the Hierophant of the Order tells Von Vampton when he envisions a Talking Android that will "Knock-It Bop-It or Sock-It" (70), meaning, in effect, to co-opt it. Similarly, when Von Vampton admonishes Woodrow Wilson Jefferson, "You still haven't made a transition from that Marxist rhetoric to the Jazz prose we want" (100), it is because his strategy requires something more relevant to blacks but at the same time diluted, derivative, not the "blee blop essence" that is "the HooDoo of VooDoo" (152). The Talking Android will be a "rapping antibiotic" whose jive talk will be the equivalent of that "antiseptic boplicity" we encountered in *Pallbearers*, reinforcing the Atonists' "Vital Resistance" (compare the "vitals"—the self-chosen people—in *The Terrible Twos*) by reducing Jes Grew's "Communicability."

It is significant that the novel opens in New Orleans, capital of HooDoo and home of Mardi Gras (the homegrown version of Carnival). New Orleans, "the amalgam of Spanish French and African culture" (6), is the place where the *"psychic epidemic"* (5) of Jes Grew breaks out again, as it had previously done in the 1890s. (For Reed, the "malady" of freedom is cyclical in its manifestations.)

While Jes Grew is being monitored by the Atonist forces, which are intent on eradicating it, its progress is also being charted and nurtured by a group of Haitians led by Benoit Battraville, who represents the Old Work (Voodoo), while Papa LaBas represents the "New" Work (Hoodoo, a more informal, made-in-America variety). It is the Haitians who give LaBas and his co-Workers the detailed lowdown on the Wallflower Order, its origins and activities; for although Haiti may be the poorest country in this hemisphere in economic terms, it is the richest in its African heritage. It is historically important, too, in having been the first black nation to achieve independence, in 1804. Furthermore, Haiti was the subject of American occupation from 1915 to 1934, that is, during the very period in which *Mumbo Jumbo* takes place.[10] This is not just another arrogant exercise of American hegemonic authority; it is also a perfect example of Atonist strategy because Haiti "mediates" between Africa and the United States; it is the crossroads or syncretization point, the regional "transmitter" of Jes Grew.

Imperialism is the logical outcome of Atonism, but the American occupation of Haiti instigated the Indigenist Movement there, in which writers and intellectuals reembraced the folk culture of the peasantry, including Voodoo, Jes Grew's spiritual matrix, which survives repression just as it survived the Middle Passage. Indeed, one prominent Voodoo scholar has claimed that the formidable power of the loas (mystères) played a significant role in the Haitians' defeat of the French armies during their war for independence (Rigaud, 49). This liberational aspect of Voodoo is certainly one of its most crucial features for Reed.

The Haitians, in fact, have a strategy that is the mirror-image of Von Vampton's Talking Android plot: they want to capture him for use as a "Great White Host" for a new "technological" loa in order to dispel the American occupation of their land (136–137). This is probably the Radio Loa with a Yellow Back which Benoit Battraville describes to Nathan Brown (151). Interestingly, the Atonists' greatest fear is that Jes Grew will reach New York and gain complete control of the radio, which would spell the end for the Wallflower Order. In the aftermath of the breakdown of Yellow Back Radio, narrated in Reed's previous novel, the circuitry has been invaded by the blues, ragtime, boogie-woogie, while in the Third World the radio becomes another "mystère." (The "broadcast" of Jes Grew is one assurance of its supremacy but, in a sense, also overwhelms its "writing." It is only in the 1960s that black literature begins to catch up with music in terms of formidability.)

The 1920s end with a Crash. (In the thirties, America is Depressed, and more people will read the comics than will read the news. Cartoonland, a region whose borders are not closed to Reed's incursions. Meanwhile, the Bomb is slouching toward Babylon to be born, while in Europe fascism is orchestrating its go for the

Grail.) Jes Grew dissipates, to partially reemerge in white culture in the 1950s as rock 'n' roll and Beat bohemianism, prior to its proper parousia in the 1960s. It never abandoned black culture, however, having served underground there for the duration. "No more wiggle and wobble" was not a slogan that carried any weight with blues people, and, consequently, it is no haphazard choice that leads Langston Hughes to call his generally sober novel of 1930 *Not Without Laughter.* Hard times do not preclude good times.

Indeed, as the title of trumpeter Wynton Marsalis's 1985 album *Black Codes (From the Underground)* reminds us, history has an oft-unacknowledged doublesidedness. On the one hand, there are the nineteenth-century Black Codes, white-enforced edicts designed to regulate and rigidly circumscribe black existence; on the other, there are the ever-present and irrepressible black codes (codes of deliverance, black "passports") that are the signifiers of Afro-American experience, the source of the contra/diction of black speech. In the end, what is heard in black literature is the voice not of suffering alone but of survival; the voice not only of outrage but of celebration: the logos of the boogaloo and the blues.

The Last Days of Louisiana Red

In *The Last Days of Louisiana Red,* Reed focuses on a dangerous potentiality in Hoodoo which he calls Louisiana Red. This is not the spice of life but, rather, an overdose of hot sauce that spoils the gumbo. Red pepper is an essential ingredient in most African cuisine, but when a Nigerian, for example, says, "Your eye go see pepper-o," he means that you are about to "taste" trouble. This negative, or Petro, aspect of Hoodoo can be traced all the way back to Reed's first novel, *Pallbearers,* in which wizened old ladies would put the whammy on someone out of spite. There, it was essentially comic; here, it is downright serious: "evilness, attitude, negroes stabbing negroes—Crabs in a Barrel" (140). This brand of Hoodoo can be useful when applied to the oppressor (the hexorcism of Noxon, for example, begun in "Cab Calloway," is still being carried out in *Louisiana Red* [38]), but among the oppressed, it can only contribute to a continuation of their oppression. LaBas attributes this deplorable circumstance to the scars of slavery, the persistence of a neo-slave mentality (Moochism), and the subtle manipulations of the slavemasters, who successfully channel the aggression of blacks against other blacks. Ed Yellings's Gumbo cure for cancer is actually directed against Louisiana Red. The metaphoric significance of cancer here depends, first, on the fact that it is the zodiacal sign of the crab, signifying the crabs-in-a-barrel syndrome that causes oppressed peoples to "climb all over" one another rather than organize in their mutual best interests. However, cancer is also a deadly disease which both symbolizes and realizes "the refusal to respond," the "anarchic" behavior of a cell (Blanchot, 86). (Cancer, like the puritanical Wallflower Order, is "unnatural"; uncontrolled growth, like that of our military–industrial complex, has clearly become unhealthy.) When Yellings is on the verge of discovering a similar means of eliminating heroin addiction, he is murdered by the "competition" (a perfect word to use in conjunction with Louisiana Red), who fear the results of an end to this form of slavery and control. (The monkey on the junkie's back is a signifier, all right, but this time not in any trickster sense; it is, rather, an image of a dependency that cannot be shaken off.) Yellings was moving from an ability to treat the symptoms of blacks who keep each other down toward a way of dealing with those external forces which operate to keep blacks oppressed and at each other's throats. As was the case with recurrent epidemics of Jes Grew, this is too much for the forces of repression to tolerate.

Having already transmuted the forms of the Gothic novel, detective fiction, the western, radio, cinema, the scholarly treatise, and more, Reed turns his artistic alchemy to drama. The particular play he chooses for his own unique manner of re/vision is Sophocles' *Antigone*, a work which has been termed "one of the enduring and canonic acts in the history of our philosophic, literary, political consciousness" (Steiner, ix). (It is worth emphasizing that the pronoun "our" identifies the *Western* tradition; it is *not* universal in its embrace.)

In *Louisiana Red*, Minnie is Antigone, Sister is Ismene, Street is Polynices, Wolf is Eteocles, Ed Yellings is Œdipus, and Papa LaBas is Creon. (Looking back to Reed's previous novel, one can already see the Greek influence at work, for, indeed, *Mumbo Jumbo* is Euripides' *Bacchae* all over again, with Jes Grew as the Dionysian frenzy and the Wallflower Order standing in for Pentheus.)

Reed's decision to structure his novel along the lines of Sophocles' masterpiece seems to have been based on a number of important considerations. To begin with, Sophoclean drama stands at a pivotal point in the development of Greek dramatic art, specifically in regard to the role of the traditional chorus. In Aeschylus, the chorus has a more prominent role, and in Euripides a lesser role, than in Sophocles. Reed views this decline in the importance of the chorus as symbolic of the decline of participation by the community in the realm of art.

Greek drama is the immediate heir of primitive ritual drama, in which there was an organic connection between the dramatist(s) and the people at large, a connection based upon a dialectic of creation and response. This dialectic is expressed through the performance/audience dynamic and also in the role of the chorus, through which the community participates in, as well as partakes of, the action.

The essential conflict in *Antigone* is between tradition and the polity. From a contemporary perspective, one might say that on at least one linked level of explication, the play also concerns civil disobedience and feminism. Sophocles appears to have left little doubt that the judgment is against Creon and what he represents, but Reed disagrees with this verdict; he views Antigone as culpable and Creon as the upholder of the community.

Given the known parameters of the Antigone story, one perhaps would have anticipated that Reed would see her as a spiritual descendant of Isis, with Creon as one of the progeny of Set. However, Reed departs sharply from our expectations in order to address himself to a problem of immediate concern: namely, psychological cannibalism. Louisiana Red, a stress plague (and therefore an antidote to Jes Grew), makes people behave in a manner similar to that which existed before Osiris entered Egypt and put man and Nature in tune with each other.

Each of Reed's novels builds upon previous works as his aesthetic consciousness keeps expanding. The comic "megamorphosis" of Bukka Doopeyduk into a werewolf via hoodoo provides the basis for the Loop Garoo Kid, a metaphysical artist overturning official history. The idea of a conspiracy to market history in one narrow, standardized version becomes the foundation of *Mumbo Jumbo*. In *Louisiana Red*, Reed picks up the problem of the relationship of art to society, first addressed in *Yellow Back Radio*, as well as a theme which may be traced all the way back to *Pallbearers*, involving the conflict between patriarchy and matriarchy.

Reed has been accused in the course of his career of being a reactionary, a homophobe, and so forth, but he has generally been able to acquit himself of most of these charges, ill-founded as they often have been. However, it is the charge of sexism that Reed has had the hardest time refuting, and not just because of the purportedly stereotypical portraits of women in his novels. I must confess that, having struggled with this problem for a long time, it remains the one position of Reed's which has most troubled me. The trouble first becomes apparent in *Louisiana Red*, and it reasserts itself with a vengeance in Reed's most recent novel, *Reckless Eyeballing*.

It is true that Reed rejects Antigone because she is a tragic heroine, and Reed rejects a tragic view of life. However, it is not true that although tragedy is a cherished genre of Western art, of which *Antigone* is supposed to be the supreme expression, tragedy does not exist in the African worldview, as is sometimes argued. Chinua Achebe's *Things Fall Apart*, for example, is a tragic novel dealing with the initial encounters between traditional Ibo society and British colonialism, and the Yoruba warrior-god Ogun's slaying of his own men under the influence of palmwine is likewise a tragic action. Minnie, as Antigone, is intended by Reed to represent those elements which prey upon the community—a problem of lawlessness, not of individuality. However, Minnie is not as extreme an example as Street, which is why he dies and she is, in the end, reprieved (after all, she is supposed to be "too fine to shoot"), but she does stand for a radicalism gone awry—as used to be said, "revolution for the hell of it" (after all, the name Antigone means "born against").

What it finally comes down to, however, is that, for Reed, matriarchy violates the natural order he has been working to articulate and redeem in his fiction. He is concerned with matriarchy as a problem because he believes it to have been overemphasized as an element of Afro-American culture; it is, in his view, simply another repressive stereotype, one whose character is more American than African.[11] It has been employed, both in fact and in fancy, to undermine the position of the black male, whom Reed believes is the quintessential victim of this country's discriminatory and exploitative policies.

Reed would say that what he is confronting in *Louisiana Red* is the problem of a rising anima, that is, of an imbalance in the relationship of the male and female principles in which the female principle becomes insatiable. Lilith, then, rather than Eve, would be Antigone's ur-mother. However, let us consider Eve for a moment nonetheless. According to patristic tradition, it is she who bears the chief responsibility for man's loss of paradise. Yet from a more progressive viewpoint, it is possible to say that though "Eve took the first bite of the apple of knowledge, it was Adam who appropriated the greater part of the fruit" (Harrison, 442).

In traditional African society, the power of women is emphatically recognized. Among the Yoruba, for example, alienated women may threaten the harmoniousness of existence through their àjé (literally, witchcraft), the spiritual force of womanhood. However, this alienation cannot be conceived of in Western existential terms; it is, rather, a reaction against improper male behavior. In fact, it is necessary for men to honor and placate women by means of an annual masquerade ceremony designed to redress imbalances (McClusky, 79). This tradition still exists, though it clearly has ceased to permeate the fabric of the culture to as full an extent as before due to the distortions and disjunctions wrought by colonialism.[12]

Antigone represents a violation of the natural order in numerous ways. She is, first of all, divided against herself (as the evil of Louisiana Red divides the black community against itself) in recoiling from her own womanhood. (Reed makes a clear distinction between being feminine and being a feminist and demands that we recognize the differences between Western and non-Western conceptions of femininity.) Second, Antigone is hostile toward men, more in love with her own obstinacy than with her lover, Haemon. Third, Antigone has no sense of humor and does not wish to listen to reason. (Reed makes these same charges against feminists and other ideologues.) Chorus—Reed's alter ego—apparently believes that (like Earline in *Mumbo Jumbo*) she is possessed by a Petro loa because he says that she has "an 'tigone on her" (54). (A tigon is a cross between a male tiger and a female lion, which brings up a subtle suggestion of a sphinx, precisely what Chorus claims Antigone aspires to be.) LaBas, however, has different ideas, refusing to believe that she is the victim of forces beyond her control; he believes, instead, that she is merely "posing as a victim of history" while simultaneously wreaking havoc (35). In other words, Minnie/Antigone is no "political prisoner" but the unregenerative element of enmity, the perpetual dissonance in the essential harmony of the cosmos.

Reed associates Louisiana Red with the Woman in the Red Dress, a classic black image of the Petro aspect of the eternal feminine. Indeed, LaBas delivers a vicious diatribe against women in the novel, depicting them as vampires and enslavers (125ff.). However, black women previously had addressed themselves to the fraudulence of this attitude; historically, they have been more inclined to view themselves as "the slaves of slaves," and they are seriously disinclined merely to assume a "prone" or bottom position in the Movement or any other context. Where Reed views Antigone as disruptive, feminists might naturally see her as "righteous and beautiful and accusatory" (Cade, 163).

LaBas's plaint that men are at the mercy of women's cunts only serves to emphasize the fact that men are the slaves of their own desires in a more uncontrolled manner than women are—a point that is more readily apparent in Delany's writings.

However, it is not only sexual desire that is at issue, for what are capitalism, imperialism, the Faustian impulse itself, if not the metaphenomena of unlimited desire? In their own fashion, Reed, Delany, and Jones/Baraka are responding at some level to the turmoil in American reality and in the American psyche resulting from what Jules Henry calls "the *first commandment* of the new era" of escalating consumerism: "CREATE / MORE / DESIRE!" (19). When Jones writes, for example, of always wanting more than is given (*Tales*, 19), he is speaking directly to the bleakness of desire, however it manifests itself. (The fact that in this context desire is linked to an ambition that is misguided in a double sense—that is, dictated by the value-system of the dominant white culture and pursued by the oppressed who aim to identify with their oppressors—only makes the implications more poignant.) It is not natural desire that is being targeted here but unnatural desire—desire that is instigated, choreographed, exacerbated in the direction of political, economic, or psychological totalization. Desire, as Reed reminds us, was the name of the first American slaver (154–155).

One wonders why Reed, who otherwise works assiduously to challenge the traditional hierarchies of power, has allowed himself to fall into the trap of vulnerability to charges of misogyny? The Judeo-Christian–Islamic monotheism that he rejects was, after all, of major significance in consolidating patriarchy, whereas the pagan sources of Neo-Hoodooism boast numerous female divinities in their pantheons; it is rather surprising, therefore, for Reed to take the staunchly antimatriarchal stance that he does. From a Third World perspective, it is probably correct to remind American feminists (especially white intellectuals) that they are still in a highly privileged position vis-à-vis women in the rest of the world who are, in far more certain terms, the "main beasts of burden" (Harrison, 438); but given this same perspective, it is even more insensitive for Reed to portray women as the problem. Who, after all, runs the world? Is phallocracy really seriously threatened by "cock-teasing" or "bitchiness"?

Pivotal to the problem of Reed's re/vision of *Antigone* is the changing role of the chorus. Antigone, Chorus complains, refuses to take his part; she is a hostile critic who causes dissension. Chorus can be identified to some extent with Reed himself, who has caught a lot of critical flak; he also can be seen as Cab Calloway, who is capable of standing in for the moon. (White-tuxedoed Chorus in the middle of a vaudeville stage before a backdrop of piano keyboards, musical notes, and a zoot-suited orchestra [26] is a picture of Cab Calloway for sure. Furthermore, his song "Minnie the Moocher" is one of the main sources of inspiration for the novel.) Chorus's attempt to find his "natural diction" is comparable to Jes Grew's effort to find its Speaking, and his inability to sell his scripts recalls the rejection of the Book of Thoth. We also have a presentiment of Reed's next novel when Chorus envisions himself as "a fugitive slave who wanted his aesthetic Canada" (54). Ultimately, Chorus is intended as the surviving remnant of traditional society as reflected in ritual (employing song, dance, and drum—like the Saturday Night Function referred to previously). Chorus is an "uncharacterized character" (161) because he represents not a single individual but the sum of all individuals as defined by the community, as the Work is the product of its Workers.

Interestingly enough, the Voodoo chorus, though male and female, is usually led by a woman (Rigaud, 120). In Brazilian *Candomblé* and *Macumba*, the *iya-lorixá* or *mãe-de-santo* (priestess) is often more important than the *babalorixá* (priest), suggesting the strong matristic influence which exists in the syncretic Voodoo sects. Indeed, the triangle representing the African trinity, with Damballah (Grand Maitre) at its apex, includes Maitresse Erzulie, the female energy of Legba (Maitre), who shares his role as "mystère of the word" (Rigaud, 93; 74–75). Just as Legba, god of the crossroads—Reed's Papa LaBas, an "old" man—has as his counterpart Loko-Carrefour, "young man" of the crossroads—the Loop Garoo Kid—so, too, Legba is necessarily "balanced" by Erzulie; the masculine and feminine principles complement one another. Reed's Papa LaBas, however, has no female counterpart as such, unless it is Josephine Baker, who is "doubled" on the cover of *Mumbo Jumbo* as Erzulie in her Rada and Petro aspects and who figures in that novel as a priestess of Jes Grew—like Ma Rainey, Billie Holiday, Bessie Smith, and Aretha Franklin (other queens of the blues, "a loa that Jes Grew here in America" [128]). The current Josephine Bakers of the typewriter, however, get no such validation; instead, Reed verbally "goes upside they haids" for being too contentious and (dare one say it?) too damn accomplished. If Reed is often *signifying*, one might say that "womanists" are frequently *audacifying* (Russ, 17).

As the reader by now will be well aware, Reed is rarely content to tackle only a single historical, philosophical, or aesthetic bogeyman in his novels, which are characterized by what Delany would term "multiplexity," and while tracing and explicating every significant idea through the mind/field of these fictions is a task beyond our present scope, it is still possible to elucidate some additional themes. One of these has to do with Moochism, another with Reed's "twisted" use of Richard Wright's *Native Son* (1940), a work with which, like Ellison's *Invisible Man*, many black American writers and critics have had to conjure.

Maxwell Kasavubu, a teacher of literature from New York (a place Reed always has viewed as a sinister, cynical power nexus) with radical-chic leanings, is one of those characters Reed calls Moochers—a group which includes Rev. Rookie of the Gross Christian Church in San Francisco, with his "mojo jumpsuit"; Big

Sally, the poverty worker with a doctorate in Black English who drives a Mercedes; Cinnamon Easterwood, "hi-yellow editor of the *Moocher Monthly*" (67); and even minor hustlers like George Kingfish Stevens and Andy Brown, two characters from "Amos 'n' Andy." Moochers are "gliberals," jive talkers, hypocrites, chronic complainers, professional agitators, "predators." One of the worst is Minnie, who—in contrast to Papa LaBas, who is able to predict phenomena through his "Knockings" (a kind of hoodoo telepathy)—has studied Rhetoric and bases her actions on slogans. "My slogans know everything. With my slogans I can change the look of the future any time I wish" (58). For Reed, Moochism describes both the life-style of parasitic elements in society and the ideology of those radical elements who cannot or will not distinguish between the true oppressed and the truly undeserving.

Max Kasavubu is one such radical. He has gained attention with his "startling thesis . . . that Richard Wright's Bigger Thomas wasn't executed at all but had been smuggled out of prison at the 11th hour and would soon return" (69). Kasavubu is a man obsessed with the notion of the "bad nigger," a figure that has served not only to "justify" lynching rituals but also to fuel the psychosexual fantasies of repressed whites (indeed, these two impulses are frequently simultaneous and mutually reinforcing). Kasavubu's fascination with Bigger as a type accounts for his "admiration" of Street Yellings, a black hoodlum who is politicized by the first book he ever reads and who flees from "Jiveass fascist Amerika" to an African country to learn "theory" (79, 97). Street is basically an ignorant punk, but Kasavubu wants to elevate him into a symbol of "uninhibited existential action" (80). One is reminded here of "Safecracker" Gould's belief that "real" black men should be "out shooting officials or loitering on Lenox Ave. . . . massacred in the streets like heroes" (*Mumbo Jumbo*, 103). The questionable masculinity underlying this sort of attitude is more fully revealed in Kasavubu's dream, in which he is Mary Dalton, about to be smothered by Bigger Thomas (150ff.). Reed uses this dream to "demythologize" Bigger, by enabling us to read his "thoughts," which are precisely the sort that Street would have: "*I wont to take that dark blue Buick with steel spoke wheels over to the South Side. Man, will them mo'fugs be mad when they see. Think I'm a pimp.*" Eventually, Kasavubu is totally "possessed" by Bigger—who does return, in a sense—and murders his accomplice, Lisa. He has flirted dangerously with the demons in his imagination, and those demons have proven to be stronger than he is. Even in the relatively slapstick world of *Pallbearers*, when Bukka momentarily seizes power, he is seized *by* power: "NOW I WAS DA ONE. . . . I WAS GOING TO RUN THE WHOLE KIT AND KABOODLE" (112–113).[13] The metaphor of disease which frequently is found in Reed, and which includes Hoodoo as a negative "megamorphosis" (*Pallbearers*) and Jes Grew as an uplifting antiplague (*Mumbo Jumbo*), also includes power, which is "catching." Politics and authority, for Reed—indeed, all forms of obsessive mastery or unrestrained over-coming—are almost always dangerous; whoever dallies with them is invoking forces he will not be able to direct.

Flight to Canada

Reed's fifth novel, *Flight to Canada*, which appeared in the year of the Bicentennial, returns to America's past—specifically, the Civil War, our most traumatic historical experience—as seen, in a typical radical departure, from the perspective of the blacks, whom Abraham Lincoln (a "player" in this pageant) termed "intelligent contrabands." Among other things, the book is a takeoff on the slave narratives which inscribe the beginnings of Afro-American literature, reminding us, at a moment when the country has cele-brated 200 years of independence, that there is, unfortunately, still something "fugitive" about black writing and black experience. It also emphasizes—as do all of Reed's writings—that history is made up of many stories, most of which have been distorted and sup-pressed in "official" accounts. Too, it again demonstrates that black experience is not uniform but has many registers.

The obscenity of the southern slavocracy, a self-styled contin-uation of the old European feudal order, combined here with the callous arrogance of present-day multinational capitalism, is em-bodied in the character of Massa Arthur Swille (*King Arthur*: the South as Camelot; *master's will*: the dominational tendency; *swill*: devour greedily, garbage), whose credo is to never yield a piece of property and who, being bigger than North or South, can "arrange anything" (38). He gives Lincoln a loan because the Confederacy fails to keep the war off his property, and he later backs a conspiracy to assassinate Lincoln because he frees the slaves.[14] Swille is an extreme example of the monopolizing tendencies Reed has portrayed and criticized in his previous works, but he is far from invulnerable. Imperial, paternalistic, incestuous, sado-masochistic, and a drug addict, Swille has Poelike fantasies which, in Poelike fashion, culminate in his destruction by the ghost of his sister, which backs him into a fire. (The slaves "help" him—with deliberate slowness—but of course they are too late. Uncle Robin has doctored Swille's will and inherits his estate.)

Just as the southern slaveholders argued against abolition because they viewed their own liberty as being ensured by the enslavement of blacks (an intolerable circumstance closely corresponding to the contemporary South African situation), Swille cannot conceive of a world without slaves. The dependence upon slavery is at the heart of the disease of mastership, a totalizing affliction. Thus the South is "the land of the hunted and the haunted" (173), and Reed's suggestion that the South did not really want to win the war but, rather, wished to be ravished (42) is an astute comment on the nature of this particular form of pathology.

Flight to Canada begins with Quickskill's poem of the same title, which he views as "more of a reading than a writing" (7), providing the same divinatory/interpretative function that Tarot cards, cowrie shells, and similar "tools" offer (88). This could also characterize Reed's work in general: what the signs point to is frequently more important than the literary/aesthetic qualities of the signs themselves. Reed basically works with ideas, syncretizing them, juxtaposing, even inverting, to create a counterview, an alternative semiosis.

Flight naturally suggests escape, the fugitive slave's bid for freedom. It is a literal flight as well, since Quickskill travels by jumbo jet, and the name Raven (a black bird) reinforces this image. We are likely to make an immediate association with Poe's raven, with his everlasting cry of "Nevermore." Quickskill, whose surname suggests both inventiveness and spontaneity, is unable to countenance slavery any longer and therefore "flies." Canada stands for the North, which was the dream of both slaves and post–Emancipation blacks—a dream which, like the American Dream itself, often proved false and elusive. In a sense, then, this is a flight to Ca-*nada*, a flight to no-where, to no-thing. Reed would have us

understand that slavery and freedom are not geographically determined, which is why we find Raven back in the South after his
"escape." Slavery is certainly not just "metaphysical," as Quaw
Quaw argues (95), but it does persist in a variety of forms.

Reed's Raven is based in part on a Tlingit Indian totem. This
allusion is significant in view of the decimation and dispossession
of Native Americans at the hands of Europeans (Reed himself is
part Cherokee), but in the context of the slavery motif in this novel,
there is an ironic relevance that may not have been conscious on
Reed's part. I am referring to the fact that the Tlingits (like other
tribes) held slaves and that during the potlatch ceremony, they were
notorious for striving to outdo one another in the number of slaves
they destroyed (Patterson, 191). The knowledge that, in Imperial
Rome and elsewhere, even slaves sometimes purchased slaves reminds us that we are confronting a problem of greater complexity
than we ordinarily are used to imagining. In the same way, we
must not fail to recognize that the victims of one overwhelming
wave of history were often victimizers themselves in another, previous wave. A plurality of virtues implies a plurality of vices; there
is no complete state of "innocence."

Uncle Robin is so named to connect him with Raven. The avian
imagery naturally symbolizes flight, and this is definitely relevant
for Quickskill's "flight to Canada," but the robin suggests do-
mesticity, and indeed Uncle Robin builds his "nest" right where
he is, in Virginia. "Robin" also may be an allusion to Robin Good-
fellow, or Puck, a mischievous folkloric figure, and to the legendary
Robin Hood, who took from the rich to aid the poor (after all,
Uncle Robin cleverly "arranges" to inherit Massa Swille's estate).

Robin is intended to be a subversive version of Harriet Beecher
Stowe's Uncle Tom. Tom "triumphs" by dying for his principles,
a martyrdom Stowe designed to be a model of Christian sacrifice.[15]
Reed has no such "theological" strategy; his Robin survives and
flourishes by rewriting his master's will. Robin, in fact, has created,
through a resourcefulness masked by a studied duplicity (the tactic
of Invisible Man's grandfather), what we might call a "Robinocracy," where freedom functions behind the facade of tyranny and
subservience.[16]

The altering of Swille's will not only provides reparations in that
the wealth of the master is now passed on, or returned, to the

slaves, it is also a short-circuiting of the process of dynastic inheritance, suggesting that the autonomy and continuity of oppression
can be broken. Furthermore, if we take "will" to mean not simply
a legal document but intention, determination, desire, then the
rewriting assumes another dimension, for the black writer's quest
for authenticity of expression, like Jes Grew's search for its Text,
implies that the obedience to masters (the canonical authority of
Western culture) has been rejected. There is a double refusal: a
refusal to be silent and a refusal to (slavishly) imitate.

In a piece entitled "Flight to Canada" which was part of Reed's
contribution to William Heyen's anthology *American Poets in 1976,*
and which seems to be a sketch for the novel, Reed offers a kind
of statement about his own career. The fugitive slave (who is also
Reed) is here named John Swell, rather than Raven Quickskill, and
it is the Porke plantation he is running from rather than that of
Massa Swille. There is even a slightly different version of the poem
"Flight to Canada," but one statement in particular is significant:
"His essays had always gotten him into trouble by pointing out to
his kidnappers, claimants, and enemies where he was at. Someone
had called him, 'A Rascal on the Plantation,' because of an essay
he had written" (266). This is important because the black writer,
whether "field hand" or "servant," has no choice but to be the
plantation rascal if the Work is to be uncompromised. From the
point of view of a society that demands conformity and seeks only
adulation and imitation from its "dependents," originality and lack
of creative deference are sufficient to incur charges of "rascality."

Discussing Frederick Douglass's *Narrative,* Houston A. Baker,
Jr., says: "Meanwhile, he bides his time and perfects his writing,
since (as he says in a telling act of autobiographical conflation) 'I
might have occasion to write my own pass' " (35). Is this not a
paradigmatic statement of the situation of the black literary artist
and his/her struggle against silence and for self-definition? It is
writing as escape: a "pass" out of subjugation to liberation, from
object to subject.

The publication of Quickskill's poem, which puts the slave-
catchers on his trail, would seem to symbolize for Reed the way
in which hostile or insufficiently informed criticism has tended to
"catch" or categorize black artists. Writing is risk, but then freedom, too, is risky. Quickskill "escapes" in his poem before he

escapes in his person. In the fugitive slave narratives, it is the other way 'round: the slave leaps to freedom, then repeats, gives "voice" to the act, in narrative.

Reed's claim that Harriet Beecher Stowe took the story of *Uncle Tom's Cabin* from Josiah Henson is consistent with his more general plaint—backed by a good deal of historical evidence—that the achievements of blacks and other oppressed peoples have been frequently expropriated by whites. History is also "herstory," *their* story, individual tales of joy and sadness, confusion and survival that constitute the collective narrative of a people. Appropriation of a people's history, Reed insists, is a denial of their identity. The slave narratives are crucial because in them black people began for the first time to speak for themselves.

There is no doubt that the slave narratives published in the decade or so prior to the writing of *Uncle Tom's Cabin* were read by and had a profound influence upon Stowe, but, as Ann Douglas points out in her introduction[17] to the Penguin American Library edition of the novel, the slave narratives had an even broader effect, suggesting as they did, through their thoroughly American heterogeneity, "a partial solution to the problem besetting American writers in the 1850s" (33). That problem essentially was one of bridging the gap "between the modes of the semidocumentary and the romance, the prosaic and the impassioned, the factual and the visionary" (31–32) which American fiction had been struggling to reconcile up until that time. What complicates matters is the knowledge that many of the slave narratives were given literary shape by white abolitionists who received the details of the slaves' lives and then molded them into a pattern of exposition that quickly became conventional. The language was frequently far too literary and sentimental to have been the slaves' own. As James Olney declares in his very significant essay on this subject,

It may be that Box Brown's story was told from "a statement of facts made by himself," but after those facts have been dressed up in the exotic rhetorical garments provided by Charles Stearns [who wrote and published Box's narrative] there is precious little of Box Brown (other than the representation of the box itself) that remains (58).

The whole project of modern and postmodern Afro-American literature is to get out of that box in terms first of voice and then of content. It is vitally necessary that one be allowed to tell one's own story. Once you find your speaking—what Chorus is seeking in *Louisiana Red*, what Jes Grew is seeking in *Mumbo Jumbo*—you still have to be able to maintain its integrity, and it is this with which Reed is so concerned. Ironically (but given the vagaries of black/ white relations in America, perhaps it isn't so ironic), this is the reverse of a concern which some proslavery apologists had regarding the linguistic contamination of polite (white) speech by black idioms (Douglas, 15), a concern that partially informs the machinations of the Wallflower Order in *Mumbo Jumbo*.

Cato the Graffado (or as Reed footnotes, both in mock pedantry and for authentication, "Sometimes spelled Griffado" [7], i.e., one who is three-fourths black[18]) is an overseer on the Swille plantation and a foil for a good deal of Reed's satire against blacks possessed of false consciousness. Cato is educated ("They gibbed me a Ph.D."), but his "learning" has merely made him more subservient to Western mastery. He calls Quickskill's poem "cute" (52) (the precise language used by at least one black critic to characterize Reed's work[19]), and he is devoted to eradicating "heathenism" among the slaves. He outlaws polygamy and arms the women slaves as a means of ensuring compliance. "They'll keep order. They'll dismember them niggers with horrifying detail," he assures Massa Swille. There is a touch here of Louisiana Red, as well as yet another allusion to the alleged dangerousness of black women that is a constant undercurrent in Reed's work. (Mammy Barracuda is another example of this; she is the "granny" of such figures as Mammy in *Gone With the Wind* and Nanny in *Louisiana Red*.) Cato is also a staunch supporter of the Nazarene Creed, of Atonism:

The women especially be thrilled with the Jesus cult. They don't ask no questions any more. They's accepted their lot. Them other cults, Massa . . . there was too many of them. Horn cults, animal cults, ghost cults, staff cults, serpent cults—everything they see they make a spurious cult out of it. Some of them kinks is worshipping the train, boss. They know the time when each train pass by. (53)

Cato can only interpret the slaves' interest in the railroad as a fetishization of the white man's technology, with the added possibility of a cargo cult fascination, whereas the reader realizes that

the slaves have taken the trouble to learn the train schedule because
the railroad is one route to freedom. Cato and Swille could never
reach such a conclusion because they do not credit the slaves with
any intelligence. Uncle Robin's deliberate feigning of stupidity is
intended to take the fullest advantage of such self-delusions of mastership. At the same time, however, there is a cult connection, if
one recalls the locomotive image associated with Jes Grew in *Mumbo
Jumbo*: "Nkulu Kulu of the Zulu, a locomotive with a red green
and black python entwined in its face, Johnny Canoeing up the
tracks" (5). The signs that are easily read by those blacks who have
not been deculturated remain totally opaque to those on the "outside," who arbitrarily put their own ignorant labels on these
phenomena.

Raven Quickskill (a stand-in for Reed in the same sense that Cab
Calloway is a stand-in for the moon) is a far cry from Elijah Raven,
one of the jive revolutionaries in *Pallbearers*. However, as Keith
Byerman notes,

> in order to go beyond rebellion, Quickskill must come to terms with the
> idea of Canada. He persists in believing that the physical Canada matches
> the image in his mind. Like Swille, he assumes no difference between
> signifier and signified. And like his master, his misreading brings him to
> the brink of disaster (234).

The actual narrative begins where the novel "ends." The last
words are Pompey's: "Raven is back!" (179). However, when we
first encounter Quickskill, he is comfortably seated at his former
master's table, dressed like a southern gentleman, on a plantation
that has since been turned into a home for "blacksmiths, teachers,
sculptors, writers" (11); he is reminiscing about his experiences.
Beginning with the second chapter, the remainder of the book is
flashback. Unlike the Wolfean notion that "You can't go home
again," Quickskill's story suggests that "there's no place like
home." It is an acknowledgment of roots. "The South in her,"
Ntozake Shange says of her character Indigo's manifestations of
Africanity (4). Just as the delta blues preceded the urban blues, the
southern rural culture of Afro-Americans preceded the inner city
experience. When Quickskill goes north, he is not only following
the Freedom Road, he is also making a journey many blacks were

to make in the aftermath of the Civil War, looking for avenues of advancement, an escape from agrarian "backwardness." However, Quickskill's return to the South also reflects a return that many blacks have made in more modern times, both as a result of changes in the South and long years of frustration in the North. It is significant that, while in Harlem, Invisible Man finally comes to embrace without embarrassment his southern peasant roots. "The roots are in my soul," as Quickskill tells Yankee Jack (151).

One's roots are in one's soul, and so they can "travel," but when one is also a son of the soil, as they say in Africa, one always wants to return to the place of origins. This is one principal reason why Quickskill goes back, after Canada, to "ole Virginny": it's the South in him.

The Terrible Twos

Reed's slaughter of America's sacred cows continues unabated in *The Terrible Twos* (1982), with Santa Claus, Christmas, Thanksgiving, the presidency, capitalism, evangelical religion, and even childhood coming under the barrel of the pen. Reed once again reminds us of the pagan roots of many of our cherished mysteries and contrasts the vibrancy of ancient ritual with the spiritual aridity and hypocrisy of the present.

The ecological and spiritual pollution Reed addressed as far back as *Pallbearers* is invoked again at the very start of his sixth novel when the earth itself has "had enough" and reacts with bad weather and volcanic uproar (3). The Northern Hemisphere begins to suffer, as if to remedy the imbalance caused by the exploitation of the Southern Hemisphere, home of all those "surplus" people the self-anointed "vitals" fear will overwhelm them (just as the Wallflower Order in *Mumbo Jumbo* feared the onslaught of "the Black Tide of Mud"). Yet Reed reminds us that even in America, an extraordinarily privileged place, there are sharp contradictions between the rich and the poor that are growing more acute now that the middleclass, which traditionally "centered" this nation and sustained its democratic principles, is shrinking, feeding the two extremes.

In *The Terrible Twos*, the Wild West is back in the saddle again, thanks to the Reagan presidency, which initiates a cold season of greed, proof that the Christmas spirit's old adversary, Scrooge, is alive and still accounting. Reagan, Reed intimates, represents a nostalgia for a bad past that was nonetheless good to the "vitals"— the Sams, Drag Gibsons, and Arthur Swilles—whose conspicuous consumption and heartlessness contrast starkly with the deprivation of the nonvitals (that is, the unfortunate many). The dangerousness of media control linked to a gluttonous and cynical power structure is made explicit in the varieties of manipulation of the Santa Claus image depicted early in the novel. When Zumwalt suggests monopolizing a single Santa Claus because as a figure he is "too dispersed," we have the Atonish strategy again. In this novel, indeed, Reed comes the closest he has ever come to Baraka's views in his depiction of the evils of monopoly capitalism (" 'The pitiful vagrants and the limousines with their shades drawn, the fascist impersonal skyscrapers' " [31]). Their critiques are similar, but Reed still does not embrace socialism as an alternative, viewing it, too, as rigid, centralizing, and Wallflowerish.

One of the ironies of the ubiquitousness of Santa Claus, a symbol of giving, is that he presides over a season of increased sales in a society most dedicated to getting. The effort to monopolize Santa is a move designed to preclude any "subversive" dimensions to the jolly old saint's image. (In this sense, then, the monopoly Santa is a kind of Talking Android, but once this figure is in place, Black Peter is cleverly able to substitute a zombie of his own creation that will undo the damage.) At the same time, religious fundamentalists see Christmas as a pagan institution and Santa Claus as a satanic imposter. Reed is clearly opposed to the "capitalization" of Santa Claus, but if St. Nicholas = Old Nick = the devil, that is all right with him, since Reed's devil, after all, is a hero, the champion not of evil but of difference. If the Pope is the policer of orthodoxy, Nicholas, like the Loop Garoo Kid, is the promoter of heterodoxy par excellence.

In *Mumbo Jumbo*, America's astrological aspect is that of a "smart-aleck adolescent." In *The Terrible Twos*, America has regressed to a selfishly infantile state—that of a two-year-old who is never satisfied and throws a tantrum until he gets what he wants. However, the terrible twos of the title are not just a two-year-old mentality; they are also the U.S. and the USSR, who have been superpower allies since 1987, when they realized a nuclear debacle probably would annihilate them both, while leaving only the Southern Hemisphere undestroyed (" 'and the world would turn brown and muddy and resound with bongo drums, half-clad people lying on the beach, carnivals, rum, gambling, Aloha shirts, mangoes, and the mad savage drumming and the strumming of guitars and everyone would live in grass huts and the world would just go to pot' " [54]—a rather blissful picture of a post-holocaust environment, actually, a world where Jes Grew could roam unrestrained yet totally anathema to the Atonist mind). The terrible twos are also a reference to Christmas Past (1980) and Christmas Future (1990), to the Second Coming, to Operation Two Birds (whose religious justification is the destruction of the forces of Anti-Christ [read: the Osirian dispensation, an un-*Settling* movement], and whose economic justification is the pruning of the human "surplus"), and, finally, to duality itself.

If, as Reed has suggested in previous writings, Africa is the planet's subconscious, those "dark depths" have hoodooed the repressed reality of America in a manner consistent with the "logic" of getting loose, of deserting "masters." (As Nance Saturday says, "Every time the black man ascends to the scene, America lets its hair down . . . Chaos is unsealed" [81].) The slaves who were carried to the New World to help build an aggressively acquisitive society in which they were denied equal participation brought with them the roots of Jes Grew, which has the power to shake the structures of Atonism. (In *The Terrible Twos*, reggae and Rastafarianism are Jes Grew's latest manifestation.) Africa is in America as a physical presence, and it is on America as a complex. In this novel, Africa as a world power finally comes into direct conflict with the United States, politically and economically, acquiring nuclear weapons and entering into the space race, thus threatening to make these "the last days of the West," a prospect that prompts the behind-the-scenes rulers of America to conceive the desperate solution of Operation Two Birds. According to this plan, New York and Miami will be nuked and the blame placed on Nigeria, thus providing an excuse for the destruction of that country. This will have the double advantage of ridding America of a large number of blacks and Jews, as well as nipping in the bud the threat of southern ascendancy and assuring the supremacy of the vitals, the so-called Gussuck race.

Although Reed's prose is nowhere near as klang-a-lang-a-ding-dongish, in many respects we could be back in the world of

HARRY SAM. Things have gotten pretty bad in America as a result of the neo-cowboy philosophy. Social security is a thing of the past; bread costs fifty dollars a loaf. Anarchism has grown to such an extent that governmental officials aren't safe. There has been an accident with a nuclear weapon in South Carolina, which has reduced the "surplus" population somewhat but has also served to make the people in power nervous. Africa is getting its act together and is "unpredictable." The white South African government is in exile on an island and keeps launching guerilla attacks against the mainland. Although some of the characters in the novel seem a bit incredible, Reed's imagination in other respects doesn't seem to have wandered very far from the possible. Indeed, when the "unbelievable" has become commonplace, the task of satire becomes increasingly formidable.

Reagan has been succeeded in office by a man who is removed abruptly for committing pederasty in public, and Dean Clift, a Ralph Lauren-style Doopeyduk, is made to serve in the presidency as a figurehead. The real power behind the throne, so to speak, is a cabal which includes a Colorado beer baron, an admiral, a right-wing evangelist, and Bob Krantz, a thoroughly obnoxious opportunist who manifests the kind of two-year-old behavior Reed is castigating in this novel. Krantz originally worked for Whyte B.C. (that is, White Broadcasting Company and, also, White Before Colored—an apt conjunction of media influence and ideology); his office was full of teddy bears and an electric train ran around his desk. He took pills and was a devotee of cocaine, which Reed calls the Inca revenge (typically, in Reed's vision of reality, excess invokes its own curse). It is coke which tells Krantz to drive off a cliff, only to be "miraculously" rescued by Rev. Jones, his former enemy, who then becomes Krantz's patron after Krantz finds "salvation" in Jesus and the sacred cause of the vitals (who correspond to the Calvinist elect, while the surplus people are clearly the preterit).

Clift, however, finally snaps out of his moral and intellectual somnolence and starts to question his beliefs. He already has reached a crisis point. The White House is haunted by the ghosts of former presidents doomed to unrest because of their crimes. His daughter, who is a 1960s-style activist, has been institutionalized and drugged to keep her from becoming an embarrassment. However, in a denouement that is borrowed (as is much of the book's plot) from Dickens's *A Christmas Carol*, Clift is transformed after a visit to the American hell, traveling there by elevator, with St. Nicholas as his guide. He returns a changed man, determined to blow the whistle on the Colorado gang and their plans for following a "cold famine of the spirit" with a quick cauterization of the festering wounds of unrest.

The situation is left unresolved, for Clift's message to the nation concerning the machinations of the cabal causes them to remove him from office by declaring him mentally incompetent, and although Reed shows us evidence that the younger generation, the children of the wealthy, are becoming members of the Nicholite underground, the "vital strain" (totally infected with the disease of power) remains dominant, and the novel ends in a typically Reedish, cliff-hanging manner. There were rumors that he was busy writing *The Terrible Threes* and *The Terrible Fours*, but, fortunately, these appear to have been unfounded or else the serial project was abandoned. Reed's next novel does, in fact, focus on our increasingly troubled present, but the focus is more restricted because it is too obviously a venting of personal spleen, a reckless endangerment of objectivity that this time can't quite make up in originality and polyhedral pursuits for its indiscretions and indifferent engagement.

Reckless Eyeballing

Reed's latest novel, *Reckless Eyeballing* (1986), seems to be an instance of the diminution of power his work of the 1980s has manifested, compared to his truly innovative work of the 1960s and 1970s. Perhaps his most "straightforward" narrative, it repeats many of his persistent concerns and reflects both his artistic strengths and weaknesses. However, Reed has spooned up so much from the same gumbo pot that, although we can still taste a lot of pepper, one wonders if many of the really solid ingredients have not been served already.

In *The Terrible Twos*, Reed has the President meeting with the leader of the American Nazi Party and the government supporting a national holiday on Hitler's birthday in belated recognition that the Führer had "prophetically" tried to prevent the "mongrelization" of the world that the "vitals" fear is imminent. In *Reckless*

Eyeballing, the Nazi mystique is everywhere. Among the items strewn about Ian Ball's studio at the novel's outset are magazines depicting Reagan laying a wreath at Bitburg, the Nazi cemetery. There is a good deal of nostalgia for the Second World War, the last "real" war (Korea, after all, was an unresolved police action and Vietnam was a defeat), and Hitler seems as "fascinating" in the 1980s as he was in the 1930s and 1940s.[20] Arch-feminist producer Becky French is promoting a play "rehabilitating" Eva Braun on the grounds that she was merely a victim, like "all" women, of male ego. Ian Ball's friend Jim Minsk, a Jewish director, is forced to witness a series of viciously anti-Semitic skits in the Bible Belt of the supposedly New South before he is murdered in a ritual reenactment of the lynching of Leo Frank. The Flower Phantom, who preys upon outspoken feminists, shaves their heads like the Resistance did to women who collaborated with the Nazis.

The irrational blend of faith, fascism, and racism that can be discerned in our society today, and which is the focus for much of Reed's righteous wrath in *The Terrible Twos*, is castigated again in *Reckless Eyeballing* and with good reason, since the problem appears to be growing more, rather than less, serious.[21] However, to equate feminists with Nazis seems to be going too far—a result of the conjunction, as is the case with Ian Ball, of the personal and the paranoid. This is not to say that there are no assailable extremes in the women's movement; demagogic, undemocratic tendencies abide there as they do in other radical sectors. Extremist politics indeed makes for strange bedfellows: witness the common cause between people like Andrea Dworkin and Jerry Falwell on the issue of pornography. Nevertheless, there seems to be a world of difference between militant lesbians, for example, and such nauseating groups as the Ku Klux Klan and the Aryan Nations. Reed himself recognizes that a distinction must be made between anti-Semitism and the criticism of the behavior of individual Jews, but he seems to have deliberately elided the differences between "feminist" and "fascist." His female characters are for the most part obnoxious, but his male characters are often drawn to them through desire nonetheless, and, indeed, these same male characters are themselves not exactly the sort to elicit the sympathies of the reader, being, for the most part, sexist and self-pitying. (Looking at Tremonisha Smarts, Ball—one cannot help thinking that his name has a deliberate sexual connotation—thinks, "she was a gasper. One of those who took short breaths when you gave it to her hot" [61]. Jake Brashford, who has long been riding out the success of his one major play, claims he has been blocked because the Jews "have stolen all of the black material, so there's nothing for me to write about" [30].) Perhaps Reed wants us to believe that these men are victims, having become what they are at the hands of women (mothers, wives, lovers, "competitors"). If this is so, who, then, is responsible for women being what *they* are?

Reckless Eyeballing begins with a paranoid dream in which Ian Ball is persecuted by Tremonisha and Becky. He has spent the night with a woman he picked up at a "non-referential" poetry reading, but she is already gone when he wakes up. Shortly thereafter, his mother, who has "second sight," calls him long-distance; she is worried about him. (She sends him checks; his IBM typewriter and Sony television are gifts from her.) He tells her not to worry; he has decided to satisfy his female critics by writing a play in which women have all the best parts. When he was a kid, he couldn't get away with a thing because of his mother's clairvoyance; now, because of those he considers feminist critical vigilantes, he can't get away with much as an independent-minded playwright either.[22] The whole of this short first chapter is woman-saturated, and there isn't much letup in the rest of the novel. Reed and Ian Ball, his alter ego, have "wild" women on the brain. They just won't give a man an even break.

It isn't clear exactly who Becky is supposed to be (a modern-day Becky Sharp armed with French feminist theory?), but Tremonisha and her play, *Wrongheaded Man*, are a rather transparent satire of Alice Walker and *The Color Purple*, which, both as a novel and as a film, has been the focus of a good deal of controversy. Reed has sided with those who condemn both versions for portraying black culture in a distorted fashion, particularly with regard to the character of black males. This is not the place to engage all the complexities of this debate, but it is important to remember the *The Color Purple* is a work of fiction, not an historical or sociological textbook, and that there can be a difference between "truth" and "reality." (Reed's novel in fact touches on this point. People keep asking Tremonisha if the sordid scenes in her play really happened to her, as if they prefer documentation to imagination.) Furthermore, there is the necessary freedom of the artist to pursue his or her personal vision uncensored, even without consensus. Reed knows this; he has caught flak himself on precisely this issue, having been stigmatized by Baraka as a "rightwing art major" because of his refusal to toe the ideological line. The conflict in *Yellow Back Radio Broke-Down* between Bo Shmo and the Loop Garoo Kid engages this very point. Adopting Reed's own stance and idiom from that crucial aesthetic argument, I could imagine someone like Alice Walker saying, "What's your beef with me, Ish Reed? So what if I write feminist? A novel can be anything it wants to be, even purple."

This debate is an old one, as Claude McKay, for one, has testified. In his autobiography, *A Long Way from Home* (1937), he relates how he told a black journalist, who accused him of betraying his race by writing about the "sensational" aspects of black life, that he "did not think the Negro could be betrayed by any real work of art" (317). I believe this assertion bears repeating.

Ball, at the sudden, inconclusive "end" of the novel, turns out to be a split-personality, even though he "grew up with no signs of two-headedness or two-facedness"(147).[23] Despite all his mother's precautions, he suffers from a curse put on him by his father Koffee's first wife, Abiahu (in Yoruba, "one who is stingy"—she refuses to share her man), who said Ian would be "of two minds, the one not knowing what the other was up to" (146). Finally, it is revealed that Ian is, in fact, the Flower Phantom (although he himself does not know it). The embittered Randy Shank, the first black playwright to be "sex-listed," is killed while fleeing an unsuccessful attempt to imitate the antifeminist avenger's modus operandi, but all of the Phantom's paraphernalia and the collected hair of his victims are discovered in one of Ian's bags by his mother while she is unpacking his things. Ball, then, is a Jekyll-and-Hyde character—on the one hand, an opportunist who increasingly eschews "offensiveness" and integrity for acceptance and "success," and, on the other, a secret personality, a "symbolic" terrorist, by night exacting revenge for the insults he has to endure by day. The combination of these two personalities makes him Reed's most negatively construed protagonist, the fact of his being an unwitting victim of a hex notwithstanding. He is, in fact, a character reminiscent in some respects of Bron Helstrom in Delany's novel *Triton*.

Both have problems relating to women, and both are problematically influenced by women. Helstrom is, to a degree, shaped by the rich, decadent women who hire his services as male prostitute, while Ball is dominated by his mother, who is also rich, as well as precognitive and extremely color-conscious. (She is a "red" woman—a mulatta—who has contempt for her darker-skinned brethren and sistren. Listening to his mother in conversation with Johnnie Kranshaw, author of *No Good Man*, Ball thinks, "Not only did the black and brown ones hate the white ones, but the yellow ones and each other as well" [143].) The self-conscious acknowledgment of African roots (Ball is from a place in the West Indies called New Oyo [the original Oyo is an ancient Yoruba kingdom in Nigeria] where they still speak what is referred to as the Mother Tongue [Yoruba?]) does not ensure positive behavior; there is no suggestion in this novel of an unspoiled vision of negritude. Louisiana Red is still around, as is its grandparent, bad juju. Ball has been balled up since birth, his psyche kicked down the Left Hand Path that Reed previously has exposed to scrutiny, while his ambition went to the Right.

Reckless Eyeballing is really a melodrama with elements of farce; it seems to have been bred on Hollywood clichés and soap opera vignettes. Most of Reed's novels, in fact, have something of this scenario-like quality, which derives from television, radio, and cinema, comic books and cartoon strips, Pop Art, and similar openly acknowledged influences. Reed is the least literary of the three authors under examination; he is, rather, a syncretizer of forms and ideas, a televisor (tell/advisor) of images.[24] His books are like old-fashioned patchwork quilts, sewn together from disparate elements of American experience as well as from the arcana of metahistory. He exploits laughter as a positive philosophy and malice as a weapon. These strategies of redress often seem to depend upon whether the artist-protagonist is depicted as a comic or a tragic victim. Bukka Doopeyduk is clearly comic, but Ball is quite the opposite—if not actually "tragic," then at least terribly flawed, a schizophrenic character who is objectionable in both personalities. As the Flower Phantom, he is an assaulter of women; as Ian, he is either ridiculous, as in his usage of Yuppie-ish expressions like "go for it" and his preference for McDonald's over German, French, or even his own Caribbean cuisine, or downright offensive, as in his hypocritical relationships with other characters or his contempt for the lower classes of his own island ("Shut up, you black monkey," he says to his chauffeur upon returning home [132]).

One might seek to defend Reed against what definitely seems to be an ad feminam argument by claiming that, since Ball is such a hopeless character, his opinions should not be taken seriously, and that, anyway, his opinions are frequently contradictory. However, escape from judgment is not so easy in this instance, for just as Delany, in *The Tides of Lust*, is able to write pornography which at the same time purports to call pornography into question, Reed, in *Reckless Eyeballing*, simultaneously indicts and "validates" Jews, feminists, "failed" artists, and so on, through a dialectical disputation between rival theories, fantasies, "facts," and emotions engaged in by various characters in the book. This allows him to make his case, in a sense, against his enemies and his "inconsistent" friends and allies, while at the same time appearing to present a variety of viewpoints, silly and serious, paranoid and playful. When Jake Brashford accuses Ball of being "nothin' but a trickologist" (106), the reader is likely to turn this accusation against Reed himself, who has, in fact, consciously identified with the Trickster figures who function at the center of his fictions. Indeed, Reed's work is a vaudeville of the spirit, a militant minstrelsy, trickster tales to trouble the conscience of a contradictory society.

Reckless eyeballing could get a black man lynched in the "old" South but is more likely to result, nowadays, in the "castration" of his career as a consequence of "sex-listing," Reed suggests. Reckless ideologizing seems to have become the ever-present danger, along with its more colloquial counterpart, reckless bad-mouthing. It is as if Reed's righteous recipe for gumbo has taken on the character of *gumbo ya ya*, a Creole term for loud, argumentative, everyone-at-once talk (Teish, 139). Through it all, nonetheless, his misogyny remains evident.[25]

Baraka credits his wife, Amina, with waging a struggle against his "personal and organizational male chauvinism" that eventually won him away from the doctrine of female subservience Maulana Karenga had made a part of his "revolutionary" cultural nationalism (*Autobiography*, 275–276).[26] Although never closely aligned with Karenga, Reed nevertheless appears committed to a phallocentric position. Keith Byerman argues that the misogyny of a text like

Louisiana Red "serves not only as an attack on women but also as a metaphor for the destructive potential within the black community; it is premised on the belief that the real vitality of black culture is male and that black women who challenge that tradition invite the destruction of their own culture" (230). It is certainly the case that such women will invite the wrath of those who are uncomfortable with challenges to traditionally held, psychologically satisfying myths, even if such beliefs are perfectly understandable in the context of longstanding efforts directed against the strength of self-image of black men in our society.[27] However, is the "real vitality" of black culture—of any culture—gender specific? It seems that only blindness or fear could lead one to make such a suggestion. Baraka has advanced on this question dramatically; Delany has never manifested these masculinist biases; only Reed remains saddled with this species of vulgarity.

I want to conclude this discussion of the "woman question" with the comments of two black men: critic Richard K. Barksdale and author Calvin Hernton. Barksdale has written

the Black man, having come out of slavery with nothing except his sexual mastery, tried to treat his women the way the white master had treated his women. That becomes very clear in *The Color Purple* and *Corregidora*. But I can also understand why the Black male writer never saw it. He couldn't get enough distance from the problem to see it with any clarity (Hubbard, 141).

Hernton, however, in his essay "The Sexual Mountain and Black Women Writers," has provided perhaps the clearest summary of the problem as well as a vigorous assault upon it. Black men, he states, "have historically defined themselves as sole interpreters of the black experience," and male chauvinism dominated even in the Black Power/Black Arts movement of the 1960s, a period of ostensible revolution and liberation (3). The works of Ntozake Shange and Michele Wallace, in particular, inspired hostility. "The word went out" that black women were being used "as a backlash against the black male's dynamic assertion of manhood" (5). What is interesting is that Reed praised Wallace's book *Black Macho* in the midst of a good deal of black male condemnation; yet his argument in *Reckless Eyeballing* is precisely the same one that was being mar-

Table 1
Reed's Novels: Time, Space, and Signification

NOVEL	TIME	LOCALE	RE/VISION ● "SIGNIFICATION"
The Freelance Pallbearers	1960s (The "cartoon" present)	Eastern United States	Invisible Man, black auto-biography in general ["Megamorphosis"]
Yellow Back Radio Broke Down	19th century The "present"	The "Wild" West	The western as a genre and Christianity as a mythos [Hoodoo]
Mumbo Jumbo	1920s 1960s Osirian Age	New Orleans, New York Egypt	The Jazz Age, monotheism, the Crusades, the Harlem Renaissance, The Bacchae [Jes Grew]
The Last Days of Louisiana Red	Present "Past"	California "Tragic" Greece	Antigone, Native Son, "Amos 'n' Andy," radical chic, American "Business" ["Gumbo"]
Flight to Canada	Civil War period The "present"	North/South	The slave narrative, Poe, Civil War history, Arthurian legend, Uncle Tom's Cabin
The Terrible Twos	1980/1990	New York, Washington "North Pole"	A Christmas Carol, the Santa Claus mythos [Rastafarianism]
Reckless Eyeballing	Present	New York, the "New" South, the Caribbean	Feminism, Nazism, fundamentalism

shaled against Wallace and Shange—that they had been "duped" by white feminist propaganda into putting down their men (Hernton, 5).

Hernton concludes by asserting that "Black feminist writers are engaged in a literature of demythification and liberation on a global scale." In their writings, we witness "the unknown coming out of the known. . . . It is the negation of the negative" (11). Reed's efforts have been cognate. It is an enterprise that demands cooperation rather than rivalry; mythoclasm is not an exclusively male prerogative.

Despite the above criticism, I wish to conclude with a reassertion of the essential importance of Reed, who as a multicultural, pan-aesthetic imagician has been working hard to counter the damage done by the image-doctorers of the Eurocentric hegemony. His states-of-the-arts are also states-of-mind; his facts, mingled with free flights of fancy, urge us to reconceive the versions of experience that we have inherited and hold dear, to trade in our *doxa* for "a new thang." In a context in which computer literacy is threatening to put us as far beyond the book as print is beyond the oral tradition, Reed is striving for a text that will speak in tongues—spirit-voices of neglected forms. Just as *Flight to Canada* is a takeoff on (and from) the slave narratives, Reed wants to emancipate narrative from the slavery of novelistic norms. For him, the signs of fiction are everywhere, not just in "writing" (see table 1).

There is talk now of appropriational art—art that is supposed to be deconstructive in its "borrowings" and its simulations, but which really speaks to the problem of originality in a replicating age. Reed, one could say, engages in a reappropriational art; he wants to take back what has been begged, borrowed, stolen, and, more often than not, mishandled. Reed is a *Mu'tafikah* raiding the "museums" of mainstream culture for hidden meanings, liberating the rainbow that has been lost in white light.

Notes

Yellow Back Radio Broke-Down

1. The reference to the possessed person as the "horse" of the possessing spirit is traceable directly to African usage. Among the Yoruba,

for instance, the person possessed is called elēgún òrìṣà, "the one climbed on by the orisha," or ẹṣin òrìṣà, "horse of the orisha." In the Hausa Bori cult, the initiate is said to be ridden by the spirit; she becomes the spirit's "mare" (Horn, 200 n.47, 190). Those possessed are also called "horses of spirits" (Adelugba, 205).

Just as the worship of the orisha long predates Christianity and is still very much in evidence, Bori is a practice predating Islam, though some European spirits have been added to the Bori cosmology (Horn, 185; Adelugba, 207). Bori has been described as "mediumship as a performance mode" (Horn, 185), and it likewise has been used by women "as a weapon for subverting male dominance" (Adelugba, 206). One might say then that oppression brings forth spiritual powers and that these powers have, at the same time, strong links to aesthetic practices (as is vividly evidenced by the tradition of the masquerade).

2. Intriguingly, LeRoi Jones also refers to Innocent VIII in *Tales*, where he uses the image of the Pope to characterize Mr. Bush, the dormitory resident, as a specific product of the West (15–16).

3. See "Blacking the Zero: Toward a Semiotics of Neo-Hoodoo." *Black American Literature Forum* 18, no. 3 (1984): 95–99.

4. Here I am punning on a phrase of Estelle Jussim's, "a tattered sign reading *Form Follows Func——*," taken from a reference to the paraphernalia of the "funeral rites" of Modernism (12).

5. Like the 1960s, another cycle of Jes Grew, the 1920s, time of the Harlem Renaissance, was a kind of carnival decade, symbolized by (among other things) the appearance of the harlequin figure in the paintings of Picasso and some of his contemporaries in that period.

Mumbo Jumbo

6. Compare the following description of creative individuality by bluesman Junior Parker, quoted by Charles Keil: "Anybody can boil up some greens, but a good cook—a good one—has a special way of seasoning 'em that ain't like nobody else's. So anybody can do it, but it's only somebody who can do it their own way" (169).

The ubiquitousness of the culinary metaphor in these various examples of black aesthetic criticism suggests the importance of a proposal of Arthur Schomburg's to examine the "ceremonial, symbolic, and African elements in black cooking" as one important index of the depth and significance of black culture (Childs, 79). This was based partly on the realization that cooking is a form of "shared discourse" (82). In Schomburg's own words, of which Reed's poem could almost serve as a paraphrase, in cooking, "no matter how ingredients are measured they must be combined with a sort of magic in order to achieve the perfect blend" (81).

7. *Mu'tafikah*, of course, plays upon the ubiquitous epithet "mutha-fuckah," which, as more than one commentator has noted, means just about everything except its literal connotation. There is an Arabic word, however, *muthaqqafin*, which refers to the cultured class. This is appropriate in underscoring the fact that these art "thieves" (thieves in the same sense that Twain's Nigger Jim is when he "steals" himself) are representatives of peoples with their own valid cultures that had no need to borrow from others in the same rapacious manner that Western culture "borrowed" from them.

8. According to Milo Rigaud, Moses repudiated Voodoo for mono-theism (14). This places him in the company of Akhenaton.

It is important to remember that Moses was born in Egypt, the land where Voodoo has its most ancient roots, while the sacred Yoruba city of Ifẹ is the place in Africa where the Voodoo divinities, the loas or mystères, reside. Indeed, the Yorubas are supposed to trace their origins back to Egypt, while the Ibos, another people of significance in Voodoo, are thought by some to derive from the ancient Hebrews—presumably from one of the Lost Tribes. Rigaud, in fact, speaks of an "Afro-Judean tradition" (45). Obviously, we are dealing with a highly complex (and controversial) heritage.

9. In English, "set" has obvious connotations of fixity; in Wolof, it means "cold," and as a verb, "to die."

10. However, our intervention in Haiti has much earlier roots. In the 1790s, America aided Toussaint L'Overture's forces against the French, but in 1806, two years after independence had been won, the United States placed an embargo on the Haitian republic, "whose continuing survival threatened the security of all slave-holding regimes" (Davis, 152).

The Last Days of Louisiana Red

11. Compare the remarks of Baraka (based on the ideas of Maulana Ron Karenga, which Baraka has since repudiated and Karenga himself revised): Black people "must erase the separateness [between man and woman] by providing ourselves with healthy African identities. . . . For instance we do not believe in 'equality' of men and women" (*Kawaida*, 24).

12. In his novel *Two Thousand Seasons*, Ghanaian novelist Ayi Kwei Armah tells us that, even before the incursions of the Arabs and the Eu-ropeans, male dominance of African culture had resulted in an excess of violence, after which women came to power. The rule of women led to an excess of abundance, which "softened" the Africans, making them an

easier prey for the "destroyers and predators." Although the reign of women is clearly seen in a more favorable light in the novel, Armah argues that the dominance of any one gender is a mistake, a failure to achieve the "reciprocity" which he envisions as being at the heart of the traditional African value system he calls "the way" (see Works Cited).

13. It may be that this is a parody of a similarly capitalized statement in Jones's *System*: "I WAS TO BE A GREAT FIGURE, A GIANT AMONG THEM" (104).

Flight to Canada

14. The assassination of Lincoln here happens on television, inevitably invoking the specter of the assassinations of John F. Kennedy, Robert Kennedy, and Martin Luther King, Jr., which were witnessed by millions not only as they happened, but in replay after replay. The present recoils upon the past in this novel through the transplantation of technological immediacy—jet planes, television, and such. Thus, there is a telescoping of time. Reed's writing has the same rapid quality.

15. The current pejorative concept of Uncle Tom appears to have derived not from Stowe's novel, but from prosouthern dramatic versions of *Uncle Tom's Cabin* and minstrel parodies that purged the antislavery content and put Tom "in his place," reducing him to a caricature (Toll, 90ff.).

16. This is of course very different from the Robinocracy described and condemned by Bolingbroke, in which the chief governmental official practices despotism and corruption behind the facade of constitutional procedures. (See Bernard Bailyn, *The Ideological Origins of the American Revolution* [Cambridge: Belknap Press, 1967], 49–51.)

17. For two other useful reconsiderations of Stowe's novel, see Jane P. Tompkins, "Sentimental Power: *Uncle Tom's Cabin* and the Politics of Literary History," *The New Feminist Criticism: Essays on Women, Literature, and Theory*, ed. Elaine Showalter (New York: Pantheon, 1985): 81–104; and Leslie Fiedler, *What Was Literature? Class Culture and Mass Society* (New York: Simon and Schuster, 1982), part 2.

18. Reed seems to have intended him to be three-fourths *white* (i.e., a quadroon), for he describes him as having "sandy hair, freckles, 'aquiline' nose" (51).

19. See the quotations on the back of the dust jacket of the original hardcover edition of *Mumbo Jumbo*.

Reckless Eyeballing

20. In Don DeLillo's novel *White Noise*, the narrator chairs the Department of Hitler Studies at an American university. In a very real sense,

"white noise"—the monomaniacal Muzak of Yellow Back Radio—is a subject in Reed's work as well.

21. The theological-political alliance of the far right and fundamentalist evangelism is paralleled by the Christian justification of slavery in the past and the present-day Calvinist underpinnings of apartheid in South Africa (where, significantly, the Afrikaaner *Broederbond* supported the Nazis in World War II).

22. The centrality of drama as an art form in *Reckless Eyeballing* appears to be based on a number of considerations, among them the "theatrical" nature of much of our contemporary reality, the "staging" of events (in particular, to attract media coverage), that link performance art with primitive ritual. ("The play's the thing," as Hamlet said.) Drama has figured in Reed's work before, from the happenings (Becomings) in *Pallbearers* to the influence of *The Bacchae* on *Mumbo Jumbo*, and the predicating of much of *Louisiana Red* on *Antigone*, and even the use of *Our American Cousin* (on television) in *Flight to Canada*. In fact, Reed has written a couple of plays himself (*The Ace Boons, Hell Hath No Fury*).

23. Reed's often abrupt and inconclusive endings, which seem almost arbitrary, are sanctioned by oral tradition, in which definitive closures play little or no part.

24. When Reed said of Muhammed Ali that "he speaks to Americans in American images, images mostly derived from comic books, television, and folklore. . . . His prose is derived from the trickster world of Bugs Bunny and Mad Comics," he could have been speaking of himself (*God Made Alaska for the Indians: Selected Essays*, 43–44).

At the same time that Reed's fictions exploit the technologies of radio, cinema, and print, they are, in a powerful sense, "patarealist." In *Yellow Back Radio*, Chief Showcase, a Native American hoodoo entrepreneur, is described as a "patarealist Indian going about inventing do dads" (38). "Do dads" is not only an American slang expression of the sort Reed relishes using, it also suggests Dadaism, one of the "pops" of postmodernism ("do dads": active progenitors, "fathers" of further action). Pataphysics is the science of imaginary solutions; patarealism, then, must be the art of imaginary realities (fictive alternatives).

25. Reed's misogyny is not his sole negative stance. His desire to "redeem" the Afrocentric spiritual/aesthetic praxis of Voodoo led him to an unfortunate "enthusiasm" for the Haitian dictator Papa Doc Duvalier and his alleged "connaissance." Duvalier claimed that his bad press was based on white people's fears that his traditional knowledge would spread among the generality of black people. Reed quotes this assertion as if it were indeed the "real" reason for the dictator's poor image (*Shrovetide in Old New Orleans*, 259). Duvalier's claim not only fits in with Reed's habitual

conspiracy-oriented view of reality but also parallels his belief that the black male is an especially hated and feared figure in the United States (144). (One of the reasons Reed is opposed to black feminists is because he sees them as participants, willing or not, in a conspiracy against black manhood.) Reed's personal "religion," however, led him into a serious error of judgment, or deliberate suspension of judgment, with regard to the Docs, Papa and Baby. He focused too intently on the elder Duvalier's interest in African culture (his voodooism) and the younger Duvalier's interest in "telecommunications" (which Reed sees as a Voodoo equivalent), while conveniently ignoring their reign of fear, their colossal greed, their despicable irresponsibility.

26. Karenga appears to have abdicated this sexist position. He currently espouses a Kemetic (ancient Egyptian) worldview that recognizes the matriarchal, cooperational nature of traditional African civilization and emphasizes the need for equality between men and women.

27. Compare Toni Cade Bambara:

"I've . . . heard feminism equated with ball-busting anger, with mental derangement, with treason . . .

"It's getting a little crazy. Brothers snarling at *Sula* 'cause Sula takes all the male prerogatives, the boldass bitch. . . . If a sister had written half the works of Ousmane Sembene, there'd be back-and-forth debates about reverse sexism: how come the heroics are always done by women? How come the women in *God's Bits of Wood* outdo the men in courage? I'm telling you, any woman who even stumbles backwards into sexual politics is going to draw fire" (Tate 35–36).

Compare also Joanna Russ, *How to Suppress Women's Writing* (see Works Cited).

In a reinforcement of the conspiracy theory that assertive black women are being manipulated by white forces hostile to black males, Reed makes Hinckle Von Vampton say: "And if the Talking Android is female she will shout before the Caucasian club, 'They just can't write, they just can't write,' but when pressed she might break into her monologue—you know the one—'My no good nigger husband who left me with these kids' " (*Mumbo Jumbo*, 70).

4

Samuel R. Delany

ASTRO BLACK

Preliminaries

Baraka acknowledges science fiction as an early influence, along with radio and cinema. Radio and film were particularly strong influences on Reed's work, too, along with television, and traces of science fiction can be found in his work as well. Samuel R. Delany has not only experimented with filmmaking, but it is evident that the sharp focus on detail in his writing is cinematic in its effects, if not its origins. The influence of radio on Baraka and Reed, however, is worth reemphasizing because it roots them in a pre-McLuhanite era, a fact that distinguishes them from younger artists who have grown up in a far more saturated media environment; it also may have something to do with the fact that their writings present characters who are known principally through their "voices," rather than through detailed description. Postmodernism indeed may have worked to eradicate the distinctions between mass art and elitist art; nevertheless, there seem to be two forms of postmodernism: "the genuinely populist, sixties postmodernism of Pop Art and underground movies and the mandarin, seventies postmodernism of continental theory" (Hoberman, 68). Baraka and Reed fall into the first category—especially Reed—while Delany, who comes out of the first postmodernist tendency, in his work of the past decade or so clearly has moved into the second category, at least in terms of his theoretical concerns (the term "mandarin," anyway, would certainly be inapplicable).

One might say that Delany's works offer an implicit answer to a question raised (not merely rhetorically) by Baraka: "What are the Black purposes of space travel?" (*Kawaida*, 31). It is not simply a matter of replacing flights to Canada with flights to the stars (although it is worth recalling that Reed's Raven makes his journey on a 747; technology does get you there—but where?). The fact that many of Delany's characters are genetically black to one degree or another demonstrates that mankind as a whole has moved out into the universe, not just one race or nation. He does not depict a future Earth as a planetary ghetto for people of color. "Space is the place. Black folks is the space race" (Goss, 250). If black writers have mapped the darkness, so to speak, of their people's invisibility, of that cultural and racial territory exploited but never truly seen by the white world, science fiction provides maps which precede the territory (Baudrillard, 253), opening space(s) for us to continually reimagine our becoming.[1]

Science fiction appears to have gone mainstream as one result of the accelerating availability of "science fiction" technology to the ordinary citizens of the advanced industrial nations. The fact that an author can begin a nonfiction work with the words, "It was the night of the last rocket to the moon" (Thompson, *Passages about Earth: An Exploration of the New Planetary Culture*, 1), is a powerful illustration of the extent to which what was once science fiction is now an aspect of history. Science fiction then is no longer outside of our experience but inside, providing a locus of speculation at the heart of a complex and often contradictory reality. It was inevitable that black writing would sooner or later engage this trend not only because black literature's parameters have been constantly broadening, but because blacks especially have a critical stake in future worlds. They constantly have had to struggle to transform dreams into realities, to redeem, as it were, the core of possibility within fantasy. As Gerald Graff has noted (though scarcely with full approbation), "The radical credentials of fantasy have never before been so widely respected" (74). Reality itself—however construed—is now so fantastic that it becomes self-parodying, if not incomprehensible, and fantasy as a genre offers an antidote of magical coherence to the rational incoherence of daily life.

In a brief but provocative essay entitled "The Fantastic of Philosophy," Stanley Cavell suggests that "in contrast to Europe's definite but marginal interest in the fantastic, America has centrally

been preoccupied with it," and asks "what it might betoken about
a culture's literature that its *founding* works are works of the fantastic?" Cavell includes, among writers of the fantastic, Hawthorne,
Poe, Melville, even Thoreau (*Walden*), defining the fantastic as
imagined journeys along boundaries or across thresholds, as well
as encounters with strangeness or otherness (45). It is this acknowledgment of otherness, the attempt to see through another's eyes
which affords us the chance to learn something new, that Cavell
takes to be a "decent answer" to his question concerning the task
of a literature centered on the fantastic (46).

If one accepts Cavell's premise concerning the fantastic and its
place in American literature, then it becomes clear that science fiction, in its encounter with the other both without and within, is,
despite a history of disparagement as paraliterature, situated close
to the heart of the American literary enterprise.[2] The American
experience itself, after all, has been an encounter, a struggle with
the other: a "new" world as distinct from the old, a wilderness yet
untamed, occupied by strange "Indians"; then the deliberate transplantation of Africans, strangers from another encounter, to the
Americas, followed by the voluntary immigration of many "minorities." As a result, Afro-American literature (like the literature
of Native Americans and others) is itself a literature engaging the
fantastic in at least a double sense: first, from the perspective of the
non-black reader, for whom the black experience is decidedly other
not because of an inherent impenetrability, but because of that ignoral which creates invisibility, or that "concern" which centers
around assumptions of "inferiority"; and, second, because the
reader-as-outsider becomes fantastic him/herself, since, as polymorphous and heterotypical as it is as a nation, the United States still
perpetuates monomaniacal, cloistered consciousnesses for whom
the experience of their fellow Americans' reality is a kind of incredible journey. It is not merely that a writer like Reed deliberately
privileges "mumbo jumbo," rerouting us to our pagan origins and
the hoodoo heterodoxy that, like the magic of man himself, "jes
grew." It is as "simple" as white people asking, "What do black
people want?" and finding the answer, which ought to be obvious,
"fantastic." This is why LeRoi Jones's declaration that Dante's hell
is heaven jolts more violently the farther away one is from a day-to-
day comprehension of its particular truth, and why the title of his

collection *Tales* is almost ironic in its simplicity; no descriptive adjective is needed for those whose world(s) these tales reflect, while the reader for whom they are "alien" will feel compelled to supply qualifiers of his/her own.

Delany uses the traditional motifs of science fiction in new, highly sophisticated ways ("the seim anew," as Joyce wrote [*Finnegans Wake*, 215.23]). His novels through *Nova* (1968) embody the theme of heroic epic; thereafter, the quest turns inward until the appearance of the Nevèryon stories, when the heroic asserts itself again, though now solidly within the context of the psychosocial. (Both "nova" and "novel" are derived from the Latin *novus*, new. Lorq von Ray's quest for the nova and Katin's quest for his novel are each transformative, although the former is a quest for power, the latter for understanding. However, power destroys, and understanding is necessarily incomplete, which is why *Nova* breaks off in mid sentence, an appropriately open ending to a book which is the denouement of the first stage of Delany's career.) Considering the difficulties Delany must have had as a black, dyslexic homosexual, it is not surprising that his works generally privilege the viewpoint of minority characters, often with an emphasis on loneliness and separation. Outsiders—frequently artists and criminals (sometimes they are both in the same person)—are important for Delany because they present a challenge to, and critique of, society's values; they test its limits. This need to call into question the givens of a particular reality is perfectly in keeping with the kind of challenges that Reed and Baraka have hurled at Eurocentrism, with its presumption of "universality." What is significant about myths, then—the stories man has made about the past—is how in large measure they have predicated what we are now living through in the present. Delany, Reed, and Baraka read back into our cultural textus in order to un-tangle the knots that tie us to our confusions and (self)enslavements.

Delany's *Dhalgren* (1975) posits a "wounded" city (dislocated somehow from the "normal" world) to which people gravitate (as they did to San Francisco, the countercultural Mecca) in the hope of attaining the freedom associated with "doing your own thing." The results, in that novel (and in the 1960s), are not what one could call ideal—although they do represent an effort to maximize human potentialities in ways other than the econo-technical, to expand rather than merely surfeit the self—for the problem seems to be not simply one of achieving freedom, but of knowing what to do with it, as *The Tides of Lust* (1973) and *Triton* (1976) also suggest. (Reed's *Flight to Canada* manifests a similar concern.) Today, there are more strident calls and supposed strategies for liberation than perhaps have ever before existed, each promising the unshackling of our dreams, our desires, our selves. Postmodern would seem to be postmythic, but, to paraphrase Marlowe's Mephistopheles, "Why, this is myth, nor are we out of it."

Dhalgren, a labyrinth with many dead ends, is divided into seven parts, the titles of which emphasize the ambiguous, agonistic nature of this city that seems simultaneously sited within our current experience and yet outside of it: (1) "Prism, Mirror, Lens"—which yield reflections, distortions, altered images; (2) "The Ruins of Morning" —a revelation of a wasteland, "broken" dawn (false start?); (3) "The House of the Ax"—a place where things are split, cut short, where we are on the "edge"; (4) "In Time of Plague"—dis-ease; (5) "Creatures of Light and Darkness"—Manichaeanism, spiritual pigments; (6) "Palimpsest"—layers of meaning, overwritings; and (7) "The Anathēmata"—a collection of fragments. The emphasis on language that began with *Babel–17* (1966) is crucial here; we are caught in a web of words in which dewdrops of manifold images flash brilliantly but ultimately only refract meaning, coherence. Art as an ordering principle, which informs *Empire Star* (1966) and is of special significance in *The Tides of Lust*, is central here as well, as are other preoccupations traceable back to *Empire Star*, a brief but pivotal work: multiplexity, doublings, *recorsos*, simultaneity.³ Between *Tides*, a work exploring the potential for containment of the chaos that desire engenders, and *Triton*, that ambiguous heterotopia in which freedom and choice are inevitably disordered, stands *Dhalgren*, an enormous effort to both summate and extrapolate the gains and losses of the 1960s, that most heterotopical decade of the present century. The fact that, as far as the novel itself is concerned, you have to go through it all again to make sense out of the confusion could be a message to us that we will have to repeat the struggles which the 1960s attempted before we will attain a clearer understanding of what really did happen then and what must happen next.

Kid, the protagonist of *Dhalgren*, is a "perpetual initiate," as Mary Kay Bray has noted (58), going through one experience after another without final resolution, without transforming insight. In this sense, he is the quintessential American Dreamer, always searching but never really finding. His amnesia suggests the "poor memory" that America's refusal to confront history has engendered, and the uncertainty as to his identity is likewise fitting in the context of a national identity which is itself ambiguous, the product of internally and externally generated illusions, so that "America" indeed becomes a concept demanding quotation marks, speaking, as it does, to so many different people in so many different ways.

Delany's galactic future, like his suppositional past, is a logical extension of the present in that the plurality of worlds reflects the plurality of *this* world. By this I mean that the dawn of civilization is really the dawning of civilization*s*, and the various cultures and states of development we currently experience are, in a distant tomorrow, equally evident on single planets as well as throughout inhabited space. If the past and present have not been uniform, why should the future be? There is not only otherness, expressed by different races and species, though with ease of communication if not complete understanding between them; there is, still, that which is radically Other. The Xlv, in *Stars in My Pocket Like Grains of Sand*, are an example. They are described as "truly alien" (93). They are the only known race other than humans to have developed interstellar travel, and no real communication has been established with them; even their starships originally were not recognized as such, being mistaken for sizable space debris. The universe remains, as Einstein remarked, stranger than we know, stranger than we can know, and man even remains a mystery to himself, despite technological and spatial advances that expand ever outward.

Delany suggests that the alien is always constructed of the familiar (*Stars in My Pocket*, 141). This is an inevitable result of the desire to "domesticate" the alien, to make it less other; it is also the reason that the truly alien fails to be understood or tolerated when it defies demystification. At the same time, Delany's past and his future, like his alternative present, are likewise forged from the familiar: note, for example, how the contemporary problem of AIDS is read back into the past in *Flight from Nevèrÿon*, or the comment in *Stars in My Pocket* (set many centuries hence) that information glut is the hallmark of the times (a comment that can be heard today). There are, indeed, frequencies of information overload in *Stars in My Pocket*. General Information may be too general; it is, significantly, poor in history (think of Reed's quip, *"It will always be a mystery, history"* [*Flight*, 8]). Indeed, one reason why the past, present, and future are familiar in many respects is that history is repetitive, nonrationalizable; in going forward, it may only be re-covering the same ground: a circular movement of ever-unsatisfied desire. The longing to overcome history is itself historical, and history, which is always in the making, is, therefore, unassailable. We are "poor" in history because it cannot be "banked on," "spent." Similarly, information, for Delany, is not the same as knowledge, which is only determined by social use. This is why "Know thyself" is still the first intellectual commandment and one of the hardest to follow.

There are no perfect worlds, for the "improvements" Delany shows us are negative as well as positive. Utopia remains that ideal state which is nowhere.[4] That there are realms of unrestriction described in Delany's writings where people are able to be as they are, be what they will, where they may seek salvation or satiety, reveals to us again and again that quests can be mere meanderings, random or inconclusive in their summations; that maximizing possibilities is no guarantee of judicious choice; that, finally, this extremity of "freedom" is a powerful revealer of inequalities. The "unlicensed zone" on Triton is, by virtue of its being unregulated and unmonitored, given every "license" for behavior, regardless of consequences.

The city of Bellona in *Dhalgren*, the UL Sector in *Triton*, the Bridge of Lost Desire in the Nevèrÿon tales, and the "runs" in *Stars in My Pocket* are fictive analogues to the Dionysian impulses of the 1960s and of the perennial underside of labyrinthian urban complexes like New York (as revealed in appendix A of *Flight from Nevèrÿon* and Delany's autobiographical *Heavenly Breakfast*). In a sense, the farther out these stories get, the closer to home they seem in their dis-ease, their sophisticated articulation of the uncertain and the speculative, their yearning for escape in dubious battle with their entrapping self-reflexiveness. When it was not merely space opera, science fiction was modernist in its heady acceptance of the ideology of ever-unfolding progress. So-called New Wave SF, or speculative fiction, is postmodernist in its refusal to automatically adopt the technological fetishes of modernism, often turning, instead, to the inner space of culture, of the psyche.[5]

The Tides of Lust

The Tides of Lust is Delany's most notorious novel. The hardest to obtain of his published works, and probably the one in which he courted the greatest risks, the book is an intense and obsessional odyssey through psychosexual zones of power and perversion, disturbing both in the revolting nature of its excesses and in the accomplished manner in which they are delineated. (Delany himself uses the adjectives "artificial" and "extravagant" to describe the novel [*Tides*, 5].) As Nancy Hartsock notes, "Power irreducibly confronts questions of *eros*" (155), a fact that Delany confronts frequently in his writings, although he might prefer to state it the other way 'round. After all, in pornography (one of the possible "labels" for *Tides*), "the desire for fusion with another takes the form of domination of the other" (Hartsock, 169).

The lineage of this sort of writing, traceable back through such authors as the Marquis de Sade, is very much of this world: penetrational, rather than interplanetary, adventures. At the same time, however, we are indubitably in the realm of fantasy.[6] "The action in pornography takes place in what [Susan] Griffin [in *Pornography and Silence*] has termed 'pornotopia,' a world outside real time and space" (Hartsock, 175). This is true even though *Tides* has recognizable sites, such as New Orleans—significantly described as "a city of many magicians" (32)—a city which has a crucial place in Reed's Hoodoo nexus. The ritualized nature of a good deal of pornography does suggest something magical, even religious; many of its activities are intended to be initiational, an induction into a certain kind of understanding (carnal "knowledge"). Yet, simultaneously, pornography is escapist, which is why the Faust myth is so important as an organizing metaphor in this novel. Proctor wants to "escape" limits, to go beyond inevitabilities of order, and yet everything that happens in *Tides* is, emphatically, "ordered." The mind can conceive more than it can command; the buck stops with the body. (In science fiction, this is not necessarily the case. In Delany's novel *Babel–17*, people can discorporate, or drastically alter their bodies through cosmetisurgery. Similarly, in *Triton*, race and gender are easily alterable, as are patterns of desire.)

Pornotopia becomes actualized in those spaces in Delany's fictional worlds specifically set aside for the practice and fulfillment of desire. In *Stars in My Pocket*, for example, there is a reference to a place for sexual abandon called an erodrome, a clever pun which reiterates the escapist nature of eros in its "flights" from the mundane, from the repressed.

A pornotopia is a kind of theater of the libido which facilitates the stagings of desire. "(love is monologic, maniacal; the text is heterologic, perverse)" (Barthes, 112). Psychopathia textualis. Again:

The text is a theatre which doubles, prolongs, compacts and variegates its signs, shaking them free from single determinants, merging and eliding them with a freedom unknown to history, in order to draw the reader into deeper experiential entry into the space thereby created (Eagleton, 185).

For the Spike, in *Triton*, all reality is theater in this sense. In *Tides*, in which Proctor orchestrates the characters around him in an effort to usher in a "new age," the same view seems operative. The bridge between the text-as-theater and reality-as-theater is the reader/participant, who, in bringing experience to the realm of imagination and in carrying the imaginative back into the experiential, ultimately changes both.

Although the Captain's early mentor, Herr Bildungs, specifically identifies himself as Faustus, it is Proctor who most obviously fulfills the Faust role in the novel. A prodigy, he follows a medical degree with a doctorate in cultural anthropology at twenty-three; by twenty-five he has exhausted the limits of erotic experience, and, thereafter, all is repetition. In India, in a brothel, he becomes a painter. (The woman who runs the house is the same one from whom the Captain purchased Kirsten and Gunner.) Proctor then writes a best-seller. Having reached so many heights of possibility, there is little remaining for him to do but attempt to topple reality itself through Faustian "speculation," the d(a)emonic energies of art thrown into overdrive. For revolution, in Proctor's definition, is the concrete crumbling before the fantastic.

Of the ritualized chaos he is endeavoring to orchestrate, Proctor says, "I'm transported by the idea of using the material in such a way that all the relations remain unreal" (170). This is Delany's own motivation in the novel. It is not the profusion of unnatural acts, including cannibalism and necrophilia, that distance the narrative from "the real"; it is the artificial "balance" of excess and explication; for *Tides* is the product of a self-conscious libertinage. As defined by Foucault, the libertine "is he who, while yielding to all the fantasies of desire and to each of its furies, can, but also must, illumine their slightest movement with a lucid and deliberately elucidated representation" (209). Language is the disciplinary force which contains both the transposed desire of the author and the articulated desire of the characters.

Dionysianism informed *Dhalgren* in much the same way that Faustianism broods over and frames *Tides*.[7] I have stated elsewhere that the "exhaustion but inescapability of myth seems to be one of Delany's main themes in *Dhalgren*," and that Kid's pilgrimage "reflects the depletion of the hero myth" ("Mirrors," 282). This would appear to be equally true of Proctor's sensual quest, which is not only unoriginal, given the long history of libertinism, but also, in the context of an increasingly promiscuous society, not very outré, being characterized as much by boredom as it is by extremism. In fact, these three features—derivativeness, dullness, and excess—are discernible in a good deal of what passes these days for revolutionary activity in the overtly political arena as well. I write "overtly" because there are also political implications to Proctor's erotic outrages, as his desire to usher in an age of moral chaos reveals. He wishes to initiate an apocalypse, yet in the world of this novel there is already inversion: license and obsession instead of freedom, lust instead of love, law without justice. The only thing really standing between these people and chaos is an artificial order based on a restless symmetry. Having already stated that the artist is the only figure free to indulge in all three of the systems designed to keep off madness, Proctor preaches, "The artist's greatest value is, like the criminal's, that he is concerned with symmetry first and values only subordinately" (123). A fascination with the criminal-as-artist can be traced in Delany's work as far back as his portrait of the post-thief-murderer Vol Nonik in *The Fall of the Towers* (1963–65), and is as recent as the allusions to the tyrant-priest-poet

Vondramach Okk, "a hopelessly privileged psychopath" who is also a genius, in *Stars in My Pocket* (1984), but an inquiry into this fascination is actually outside the limits of this study, except to note it as an analogue to Proctor's thesis. It is also necessary to add that the concept of symmetry as an important aesthetic index is not found in all cultures—African art, for example, places greater emphasis on rhythm and vitality—and neither is the idea of the amorality of the artist a universally accepted one. It seems significant, then, that the Middle English meaning of *proctor* is agent or deputy, suggesting that Proctor may be playing Mephisto to his own Faust, articulating those proverbs of hell that appeal to the intellect while offering damnation to the spirit.[8]

Tales of the Modular Calculus

Delany's "Informal Remarks Towards the Modular Calculus" have so far appeared in five parts. The novel *Triton* comprises part 1; appendix B to *Triton*, part 2; the appendix to *Tales of Nevèrÿon*, part 3; the novel *Neveryóna*, part 4; and appendix A to *Flight from Nevèrÿon*, part 5. The modular calculus, then, embraces both science fiction and fantasy, as well as critical/confessional modes.

"Modular" is the adjectival form of "module": allotted measure, but also allotted power or capabilities, suggesting that a modular calculus, as Delany employs it, facilitates the "mapping" of culture as both creation and definition. A second meaning of "module," as the design in little of some larger work, underscores the way in which Delany has spread his "informal remarks" across four books so far (three of them constituting an actual trilogy). Furthermore, the archaic meaning of "module" as pattern or exemplar reinforces the above, while an obsolete usage of the word as a verb, meaning to sing or perform, to mold, reminds us that we are in the realm of art. Gregory L. Ulmer argues that a postmodern pedagogy can be "facilitated by a retracing of the paths" that have already been "breached" by the arts (168). Delany's modular, then, using art as its vehicle, would seem to be a tool or technique of postmodern pedagogy.

Since a modular system allows routes back to the system being modeled, we could view black experience itself as a modular in the sense that we can trace both the routes and the roots of that experience. Black artists and scholars, in the face of disrupted or distorted traditions, are engaged in an effort to redeem the arche-trace of black essences, especially within the realm of orality and the visual. Delany's concerns are perhaps more textual, but it is important to remember that for him, writing is a very broad concept, a heterogeneous semiosis, as it is for Reed. Indeed, for Delany the double lesson of civilization is its breadth and complexity. This is precisely Reed's point in attacking the reductive monism of the Atonist creed. There are many "writings," many "texts," many "voices." This is why, in Delany's work, the past is more than prologue; it is analogue or, better, anaglyph. An anaglyph is a picture consisting of two slightly different perspectives of the same subject in contrasting colors that are superimposed on each other. The astrolabe, which appears again and again in the Nevèrÿon stories, is important for the same reason: one matrix is superimposed on another, and both are necessary for a correct "reading." The fact that the astrolabe is sometimes called the world's oldest scientific instrument may provide an additional clue to its significance as a symbol in these tales, writings in which the business of origins is everywhere insisted upon. Furthermore, the astrolabe is a navigational tool, which is also fitting in a context of various forms of quest.

Some Informal Remarks Toward the Modular Calculus is the title of metalogician Ashima Slade's Harbin-Y lecture series, discussed in appendix B of *Triton*, and the title of the first lecture in the series, "Shadows," is one that Delany himself used for a speculative/critical essay. As Slade's "editor" tells us, Slade took the title "from a nonfiction piece written in the twentieth century by a writer of light, popular fictions: it employed the same galactic presentation and the term 'modular calculus' appears (once) in it" (357). By this kind of self-referential play, Delany is able to both blur the boundaries between "fact" and "fiction" and create a future which draws upon a "history" of which his own work is a part. Frequently, Delany enables us to trace ideas and allusions back to other books: for example, the Sygn, a religious sect "practicing silence and chastity" (*Triton*, 346), and supposedly wiped out in the destruction of Lux on Iapetus during the war between Earth and the Outer Satellites, appears again in *Stars in My Pocket* as one of the two contending forces for domination of the inhabited worlds. Bellona, the city on Mars which is the birthplace of both Ashima Slade and Bron Helstrom, has the same name as the city which provides the locus for action in *Dhalgren* and which is situated exactly in the center of the United States. Again, elements of the world depicted in the Nevèrÿon stories are present in the "vlet" game played by some of the characters in *Triton*.[9] Slade's admonition to her students to "construct alternate models from these ideas" (*Triton*, 352) would seem to be a statement of Delany's own practice.

In the appendix to *Tales of Nevèrÿon*, Delany gives us details of the Culhar' fragment upon which his tales have been predicated, as well as biographical information on its translator, K. Leslie Steiner, a brilliant linguist/mathematician who also dabbles in science fiction criticism. (Steiner is the putative author of an essay on *Tides* as "anti-pornography." The essay, though unpublished, exists, but Steiner, like the Culhar' fragment, is an invention of Delany's. She is one of a number of remarkable women he portrays, like Rydra Wong in *Babel-17* and Venn and Raven in the Nevèrÿon stories. Delany's protagonists often are aided or tutored by women, and it is often women who provide the crucial breakthroughs in knowledge or understanding in his fictions.) We are told that there is one particular phrase that has "puzzled commentators" because, as Steiner interprets it, there are at least three different but equally possible versions:

1. "The love of the small barbarian slave for the tall man from Culharē"
2. "The love of the tall slave from Culharē for the small barbarian"
3. "The small love of the barbarian and the tall man for slavery."

Steiner believes it possible that the phrase is a pun which embraces all three of these meanings but does not explain "how this might actually function in the narrative" (261). The reader of the Nevèrÿon trilogy, however, will know that Delany uses all three meanings himself to generate one of the principal strands of his plot: the story of Gorgik the Liberator, his intimate relationship with Small Sarg (and later with Noyeed), and the struggle against chattel slavery, complicated by the enslavement to desire.

Small Sarg is sexually turned off by wearing the iron slave collar, but one or the other of them must wear it in order for Gorgik's desire to be freed, for he cannot make love "without some mark of possession" (*Tales*, 143).[10] This, apparently, is one aspect of the complexity that servitude generates, which is a reverse image of the complex relationships of mastery, where the enslavement is to power (24). What is freedom; where is it? As Small Sarg says to Gorgik, tellingly: "Every time I think I am wearing one chain, I only find that you have changed it for another" (143).

Early on, we are told of Gorgik that he had been "stripped to nothing but his history, *and now that history included their evaluations of him*" (*Tales*, 27; my emphasis). It takes no great leap of imagination to see the relevance of this statement to the black experience, in which the fictions that Europeans created about Africans indubitably have "colored" their history, in largely detrimental ways. "The gesture of reaching out to the most unknown part of the world and bringing it back as language . . . ultimately brings Europe face to face with nothing but itself, with the problems its own discourse imposes" (Miller, 5). One might say that in reaching out to a distant, suppositional past and bringing it back as language, Delany brings that past face to face with the present, with the limits of our discourse and the constancies of our experience, its changing sameness."[11]

One thing that adds poignancy and complexity to the statement quoted above about Gorgik's history is that those doing the evaluating are the Child Empress Ynelgo, whose seizure of power coincides with Gorgik's enslavement, and members of her court, to which he has been brought by the Vizerine Margot.[12] Ynelgo is black, as are many of Nevèrÿon's aristocrats. So is Gorgik. At the same time, there is a reference in *Neveryóna* to "blonde, nappy-headed, blue-eyed chattels" (288; compare the description of Marq Dyeth in *Stars in My Pocket*). For Delany, who never takes a simplex view of anything, slavery is not a problem tied exclusively to race, as the particular nature of slavery in the Americas often leads us to assume. Slavery is basically a power relationship, and it is also economic, for, as Orlando Patterson notes, slaves were "the earliest article of trade" (148).

Patterson argues that "before slavery people simply could not have conceived of the thing we call freedom"; that, paradoxically, it is the slave's desire for "disalienation" that creates the idea of freedom (340). It is perhaps in this sense then that Gorgik, in his role as "the Liberator," is most significant; he does not bring freedom itself but the idea of freedom to those for whom it may serve as an inspiration.

In *Flight to Canada*, Reed showed us that while slavery is real it has many forms and that "Canada," finally, is a state of mind. Delany, too, shows us different forms of slavery, as symbolized by the various meanings of the collar, an ambiguous "sign," the wearing of which, however, is the mark of one form or another of un-freedom. However, in the context of civilization, these equations become increasingly complex. Indeed, futuristic though it is in many of its concerns, Delany's fiction nevertheless frequently privileges the primitive as a "natural" state compared to the "rough, brutal, and inhuman place they call civilization," with its "repressive toils" (*Tales*, 130, 158). Gorgik, in his long monologue to Pryn as they wander through the market in the third chapter of *Neveryóna*, refers to "those bournes where civilization has not yet inserted its illusory separation of humans from the world which holds them" (51)—another sort of alienation—and admits that he himself is "a slave to all the forces" of civilization's "flow and form," whereas Pryn's own "freedom" indicates her ignorance of the forces that compel her (53–54).

Social knowledge, coupled with self-knowledge, makes one more aware of the limits of freedom but also frees one from naive and possibly dangerous delusions. Consider the case of Bron Helstrom, Delany's troubled antihero in *Triton*, who suffers precisely because he does not have Gorgik's kind of ruthless but realistic insight. Bron is a character whose twentieth-century style machismo and misogyny are very much out of place in the egalitarian twenty-second-century society in which he lives.[13] He thinks he is "reasonably happy" and "happily, reasonable" (1), but he is wrong on both counts; the Spike, when she first meets him, calls him "confused" (14). He takes pride in being contrary to what he takes to be the norm, which he imagines makes him unique, whereas he is only another "type," according to his friend Lawrence (7). It is symbolically apt that when he enters an ego-booster booth to view a randomly selected few minutes of audiovideo tape of himself, there is a malfunction. "KNOW YOUR PLACE IN SOCIETY," the booths proclaim. However, all Bron gets is a blur and a buzz.

Bron moves into his men's co-op to get away from women and sex, but he can't; his accidental but crucial encounter with the Spike triggers an obsession. As a male, Bron is (or desires to be) the possessor; as a female, after a sex change, she offers herself to be possessed, but this is only an extreme ploy to achieve, in a radically reversed fashion, the possession of the Spike that remains a persistent goal. Bron can alter *him*self to *her*self but cannot cease to be the unbalanced personality s/he is.[14]

Delany's Nevèrÿon trilogy is a fantasy based on the project of Foucaultian archaeology, which explores the transformations that constitute change and grounds these to a great extent in power and the body ("bio-power"). The focus is on desire. Foucault schematizes desire as an ethical problem which is triangular in structure—acts, pleasure, desire—with the emphasis shifting according to the culturo-historical perspective. According to Foucault, it is desire which is in the ascendant at present, "since you have to liberate your own desire. Acts are not very important, and pleasure—nobody know [*sic*] what it is!"(Dreyfus and Rabinow, 242–243). There is a good deal in this assertion of Foucault's that is relevant not only for the Nevèrÿon stories, but for the circumstances, situations, and personalities in *Triton*, *Tides*, and *Dhalgren*, as well.

Delany opens *Tales of Nevèrÿon* with references to Derrida's concept of the provisional authority of the text and Said's view of beginnings as speculations about the unknown, then confronts the reader in the first few pages of the initial story with a number of doublings: slaves, male and female, elegant and ragged, all wearing the iron collar that denotes their chattel status; Gorgik's "double memory" of money and writing (both employing "coinages"); the primitive and the sophisticated responses (terror, ignoral) to those phenomena with which neither high nor low language can deal. Later, we are told by Venn that money and speech are mirrors—methods of exchange, of speculation; indeed, money creates images, while writing can be used to control slaves.

All of this seems a long way from the province of fantasy, but these depths, this misalignment of expectation on the part of the reader with the "rewards" of the text, are deliberate. One similarity between Reed and Delany is that they have both worked to gain respect for previously disparaged literary forms. Their efforts are an emphatic reminder that "seriousness" is not the prerogative of canonized texts alone and that there are many forms of mastery.

Not only are the Nevèrÿon tales about ideas, but the scholarly epigraphs serve to make these ideas all the more insistent, bracketing an often-denigrated paraliterature (fantasy) in the context of post-modern theory (which also provides the subtext).[15] The tales elaborate, demonstrate, the theoretical statements: a situation of language reflecting upon language. (This is speculative fiction, it is important to note again: from *speculum*, mirror.) The action, such as it is in these tales, is to a large extent the stock action of sword-and-sorcery. Apart from this, nothing really happens but an intricate dance of meanings, a weaving of reiterated themes into a splendidly detailed tapestry, grammatological in nature, about writing in all its various senses. We do not watch the story unfold, we watch the language unfold; it is that unfolding which is the story.[16]

Quickly, too, however, we do encounter the fabulous: dragons. The past, for Delany, is magical as well as functional. In the world of the imagination, there is no conflict between dragons and writing, for the latter inscribes the former. The action of materially creating a culture and the action of dreams and desires interpenetrate; desire, indeed, instigates praxis.

In *Neveryóna* in particular, dragons can be both mundane (a creature one rides) and amazing (Gauine)—like writing itself. Therefore, dragons exist as a multiple signifier: the dragon as an index to magical reality, a somewhat conventional role ("Here there be dragons" traditionally has connoted the unknown), and the dragon as a realized commonplace within the world evoked by the text. Dragons are "fantastic" to the reader but familiar to Pryn, who has tamed one, and familiar, too, to the reader by the time both encounter Gauine, when the fantastic reasserts itself.

The opening metaphor of the Culhar' fragment, which provides the basis for a recurring motif in these stories, is of sunken towers "inscribing their tale on the undersurface of the sea," so that sailors looking down into the water could read it. One of K. Leslie Steiner's "emendations," Delany tells us (through S. L. Kermit, "author" of the appendix to *Tales*, and another of Delany's scholarly critical alter egos), is that this is an image of signs of hidden obstacles to be avoided (259). Melding the two readings, one can derive a message about the "subsurface" meanings of the past and a suggestion that, properly read, history can steer us away from the dangers man has faced previously but, through ignorance or arrogance, keeps reencountering.

The ancient city of Neveryóna, referred to as "just a pattern in the water that shows up under the proper light" (*Neveryóna*, 300), is itself a metaphor for the way in which vestiges of the past can be read and interpreted (reconstructed); the "proper light" is one's perspective. "To write is perhaps to bring to the surface something like absent meaning" (Blanchot, 41; compare Jones's "drowned mandala" [*System*, 20]). In the discussion of excluded meanings that takes place between Pryn and the Earl Jue-Grutn (313), the "engine" referred to, which can open spaces for the entry of what has been excluded, is language. One might say that it is the language of power, or the way in which power controls or asserts itself through language, but it is also the re/creative power of language. In any event, it is surely tied to history and has a great deal to do with those who determine history and those whose history is determined by the ones with the means of controlling it, who hold the light, as it were, that illuminates what is obscure. African reality, for example, was not read or seen in the proper light by European colonizers, who demonstrated an inability or a refusal to interpret the signs of the African past, preferring to assert that Africa had no history. Hence the signature, or sign-nature, of reality is crucial for Delany. History signs itself in various ways and, at the same time, may be assigned.

In the epigraph to chapter 11 of *Neveryóna*, there is a quotation from Novalis: "Writings are the thoughts of the State; archives are its memory" (267). This is relevant not only to Delany's work but to Reed's as well. If, originally, writings are "the thoughts of the State," then the appropriation of writing by the forces of the imagination becomes commensurately more significant and by definition political, for writing is then either a critique (explicit or implicit) of the State or an alternative to it through the creation of fictional worlds. This is why Plato wished to banish poets from his Republic. For Delany, "origins are . . . always contouring ideological agendas" (*Flight*, 368). Organization of the past through the writing of history, through the reading of history (both as decoding and as interpretation) is a crucial enterprise. The Earl Jue-Grutn complains of the difficulty of keeping the past organized, claiming that when it is disorganized, the present will be "barbaric splendor—and misery" (*Neveryóna*, 315). For the Earl, however, organization is equivalent to control. Control of the past helps to consolidate control of the present. This is one reason why Gorgik is so feared in his role as Liberator: for the eradication of slavery is not only a radical reorganization of society, it is, preeminently, the elimination of one totalizing means of control. Furthermore, the tighter the organization, the less freedom, which is why Delany concerns himself with examining overdetermined systems (in *Stars in My Pocket*, the universe itself is seen to be overdetermined [161]). The routes of adventure often lead away from civilization or through civilization's interstices, and imagination provides the map (as well as alternative agendas). Thus Pryn, at the end of *Neveryóna*, gazes at high banks of cloud shaped like towers and terraces and declares to herself, "*That's* the city you must learn to read. . . . That's the city you must write your name on—before you can make progress in a real one" (362–363).

It is interesting, too, that when Pryn has her first "writable thought," it is of a makeshift, horse-drawn cart with ornate carved designs that appears to her as "an over-sized reproduction of something yanked from the earth, a rootish knot with all sorts of excrescences, off-shoots, and out-juttings" (270). This organic image is not only appropriate in the context of a society still in transition from an agricultural base to a more technological, urban one; it becomes, as well, a metaphor for art itself—especially an art concerned with roots (why-knots), with "changeable mysteries" (362).

Regarding black writing, the importance of understanding or having an organizational viewpoint or metaphor for the past is crucial, because for blacks, as for many oppressed peoples, the past has either been distorted or obliterated or written over by the oppressor in ways that need to be examined carefully and redressed. Official history, after all, is a colonization of the past by the present, ordering and interpreting the flow of ideas and events according to its own strict schemes. It is not only the future that harbors possibilities; the past, too, holds untried alternatives as well as failed struggles. By reexamining our origins, we can recontour our ideological agendas. This is a strategy understood very well by all three of the authors under consideration in this study.

In *Neveryóna*, Delany views certain inventions or solutions to problems—which are discovered, lost, and rediscovered—as coinciding with moments or peaks of civilization, a rising/falling or cyclical movement, not a steady linear progress. What goes around, comes around. Also, the "authorship" of civilization is seen to be multiple (and sometimes simultaneous); it is not the "property" of the genius of any particular race or gender. Mankind as a whole may have descended from one ur-mother, but, culturally and creatively speaking, our origins are plural.

Within this novel, stories themselves have alternative endings or exist in various versions attributable to different storytellers. The tales Pryn hears or re/tells are in some cases the very ones she finds herself living out. Furthermore, since many of the ideas in the text are based on speculations concerning the origins of culture, on writing and civilization, drawn from other(s') texts, even the authorship of the Nevèrÿon tales becomes, in a sense, multiplicitous or certainly more than individual, Delany being the one who binds together (or weaves) in his own particular style the strands he has borrowed as well as imagined, as his second appendix to *Neveryóna* seems to suggest. Even the author is to some extent a fiction.

Women characters largely dominate the Nevèrÿon trilogy: the Vizerine Margot, the Child Empress, Venn, Raven, Norema, Pryn, Madame Keyne, and others.[17] Male characters of importance are fewer and frequently homosexual—Gorgik, Small Sarg, Noyeed—while Jahor is a eunuch, though the Earl Jue-Grutn and his sons, among others, are heterosexual. Although, because of his wide-ranging experience, Gorgik is "the optimum product of his civilization" (*Tales*, 54), Delany makes it clear that women have had a large hand in civilization's development and transmission. One feminist scholar has declared in fact that women are "the literal and material producers of men, who like to imagine that the situation is the reverse" (Hartsock, 277). Delany's gynocratic creation myth, narrated by Raven, reflects this concept of the matristic preceding the patristic.[18] This genesis, in which Eif'h is punished by god and becomes " 'man," meaning "broken woman," "no longer she, but 'he, as a mark of her pretention, ignorance, and shame" (*Tales*, 174), is a complete reversal of the Freudian view of woman as "imperfect (castrated) man" (Ann Rosalind Jones, 364; Kristeva, 40). The gynocentric universe is spoiled when harmony is reduced to a single melody, for diversity is praise (*Tales*, 173). Woman is reduced to 'man, and the fall of Paradise ushers in the rise of the phallus. Thus Raven, who is from a matriarchal society in the Western Crevasse, sees Nevèrÿon as a "strange and terrible land where men aspire to woman's place" (*Flight*, 90). One suspects that in the world of these tales matriarchy is an exception rather than the rule, but its significance is measured by a recognition that for "hundreds of thousands of years the culture of women and women's mysteries had been the dominant ideology of humanity" (W. I. Thompson, *The Time Falling Bodies Take to Light: Mythology, Sexuality, and the Origins of Culture,* (156). This "feminization" of the past is reasserted in the future in *Stars in My Pocket,* where all people, regardless of gender, are known as "women." (In *Tales,* Raven calls Bayl, who is male, a "daughter" of Eif'h [192].)

Madame Keyne, who is the developer of the New Market in Kolhari and hence an apostle of "progress," nevertheless worries that her society will lose all contact with magic and that when this happens it will be necessary to use "other signs entirely" to write about civilization (*Neveryóna,* 145). That this is an accurate "prediction," we know from our present perspective. It is to get back to the magic signs that is Reed's particular endeavor. Even though the Nevèrÿon tales are ostensibly sword-and-sorcery, there is actually very little "sorcery"—despite the presence of dragons, despite Pryn's "conjuring" of the drowned city of Neveryóna.[19] What magic there is in this realm already has largely "migrated" to the inventions of civilization-in-the-making: things like the astrolabe, like Madame Keyne's fountains, like money. (Money, indeed, is a newer, more efficient form of slavery; the iron from disused slave collars is melted down to make the coinage with which Madame Keyne pays her laborers. Money becomes a new "circle" of desire.) Magic, as Madame Keyne explains to Pryn, is power, and now power has become like magic, working its own transformations.

Pryn, the heroine of *Neveryóna,* is initially called "pryn" because, prior to meeting Venn, she knew how to write but had no knowledge of capital letters. Writing without capitals is a form of innocence. Capitalization brings forth "proper" nouns, a different class of words and letters that destroys equivalency; capitalization, too, suggests the connection between writing and economics. Pryn's name also suggests Hester Prynne, who wore the letter A (alpha, the Adamic letter, though ironically designating a daughter of Eve), which she managed to appropriate for art and independence, despite its being forced upon her as an intended stigma by a puritanical, patriarchal society. The fact of gender-specific interpretations of meaning is depicted in a different way in *Neveryóna* with reference to the word *nivu*—from *chatja nivu*, meaning a house where women refuse to cook for men but generally referring to "any lack of support a woman may show a man" (101). From a feminist perspective, this word is positive, a statement of necessary limits to male dominance in a society where men take everything from women (169), but, not surprisingly, *nivu* has become a dirty word from a masculine perspective. Female independence means a "pollution" of male power.

It is not possible within the fairly strict limits of this work to do anything like full justice to the complexity and sophistication of Delany's fiction. In my discussion of those writings linked by the "algorithm" of the modular calculus, I have simply sought to offer some wide-ranging remarks in keeping with the focus I have tried to maintain throughout this study as a whole, dealing with patterns of desire, with black culture as a rich continuum, and with black postmodernism as a simultaneously resurrectional and contra/dictional enterprise, engaged in freeing blackness from the vexations of an imposed history and at the same time celebrating the roots of black becoming.

It is surely significant that Delany "creates" the modular calculus in the future, in the novel *Triton*, where the societies on the Outer Satellites, extensions of Earth culture(s), are struggling for true independence, just as many nations of the Third World today are striving to escape the embrace of neo-colonialism. The roots of that future conflict between the home world and the moons can easily be traced to our real historical blunders/plunders and current inequalities. From the West against the rest, it is a simple temporal leap to the Earth against the rest and, eventually, humankind itself against the Other(s).

However, this is a pattern of struggle that is older than the West; it goes all the way back to man's original desire for mastery—which is why Delany moves back with his calculus, his "guiding grammar" (*Flight*, 376), to Nevèrÿon (a never-ever land of manifold significance), to the beginnings of the "engineering" of power, of sexual interaction, of language itself, of all those mechanisms in which we are still complexly enmeshed. Just as Bron Helstrom's difficulties can be rooted in our current malaise, which his own twenty-second century has not resolved but merely overdetermined, our own anxieties and entrapments can be seen in the endless quest, endlessly unresolved, of Gorgik and others like him for "freedom." Afro-Americans were emancipated from slavery, but are they "free"? African states achieved independence from their former colonizers, but are they "liberated"? The United States declares itself to be "the home of the free," but is the nation itself in control of its own impulses, of the accelerating energies that drive it toward the satisfaction of its enormous desires? Reed was very astute in calling Happenings "Becomings" in *Pallbearers* because the answer to that by-now-ritual query, "What's happening?," is, "We're (still) becoming." This is the imperative we are all slaves to, unless we make an end of ourselves.

Stars in My Pocket Like Grains of Sand

Stars in My Pocket Like Grains of Sand is the first volume of a diptych of novels, the second of which, *The Splendor and Misery of Bodies, of Cities*, is forthcoming. The conjunction of the erotic and the urban which the latter title suggests is actually an always-present fusion in Delany's work. In a recent essay, William H. Gass writes, "In knowing a city—its inhabitants and areas and objects—only the carnal sense of 'know' applies" (38). The city is both an expression of, and a focus for, desire. This is validated again and again in Delany and, beginning with that explicit triangle of novels (*The Tides of Lust, Dhalgren, Triton*), with an almost allegorical intensity.

It is desire, indeed, which specifically informs this novel. In *A Lover's Discourse: Fragments*, Roland Barthes writes, "The other with whom I am in love designates for me the specialty of my desire" (19). Barthes then quotes Lacan: "It is not every day that you encounter what is so constituted as to give you precisely the image of your desire" (20), yet it is this very circumstance upon which a significant aspect of the plot hinges. Marq Dyeth, an industrial diplomat, a man of learning, privilege, and sophistication, and Rat Korga, sole survivor of an utterly destroyed world which he had known only from the most impoverished perspective, turn out to be each other's perfect erotic object.

The cliché about people being from "two different worlds" is literally true for them, although it has, as well, a more emphatic meaning in this vast interstellar context. Rhyonon, Rat Korga's world, which destroys itself as a result of Cultural Fugue (socioeconomic pressures and technological perturbations that lead to an annihilating instability), is very different from Marq Dyeth's planet, Velm. On Rhyonon, an older language is spoken in which men and women are referred to as "he" and "she," or "dogs" and "bitches," whereas in more progressive regions of the galaxy, males and females alike are referred to as "women" and denoted "she"; the masculine pronoun is used to indicate sexual interest, not gender. Rhyonon also, for religious reasons, has resisted linkage with General Information, a system allowing practically instantaneous mental access to all available data. (GI is the invention of an organization known as the Web, which controls the flow of information between worlds but discourages interstellar travel. The Web—whose personnel are known as Spiders—"intervenes," on occasion, in the affairs of individual worlds that are experiencing extreme difficulties.[20] It is the Web, too, which instigates the meeting between Dyeth and Korga.) Rhyonon also practices Radical Anxiety Termination—the procedure that Korga undergoes (the appellation "Rat" comes from the acronym RAT)—a form of "mental suicide" that originally was a rite in a political movement, later a violent artform, and finally a form of "public philanthropy" designed to deal with sociopaths from the planet's slums. RAT involves jamming the same synapses used to connect the mind with GI and is illegal on most worlds.[21] Korga volunteers for this procedure because he has a desire for knowledge and for happiness, and, since prenatal brain damage has made the former difficult for him to achieve, he accepts the latter. " 'Of course,' they told him in all honesty, 'you will be a slave. . . . But you will be happy' " (3).

It is not clear what sort of government Rhyonon has, although there is a struggle between the reactionary Grays and the radical Free Informationists prior to the fatal holocaust. Velm, however, practices bureaucratic anarchy, most popular of the different forms of world government among the 30 percent of the more than 6,000 inhabited planets that have them, and which include syndicated communism, benevolent feudalism, oligarchic collectivism, and industrial fascism. Bureaucratic anarchy is socialism that experiences temporary but persistent rashes of capitalism. Although an anarchic bureaucracy would seem to be horrendous form of government, we have no negative portrait of it in the novel, a good deal of which takes place on Velm, but this may be due to the fact that Marq Dyeth is really a kind of aristocrat and his family seat, Dyethshome, a very privileged retreat. From the above list, however, it would seem that the idea of world government has not worked out extremely well, which may be the reason 70 percent of the planets do without one.

Still, Velm is a far more progressive world than Rhyonon, though it is not uniform in its achievements. Relations between humans and evelmi (the indigenous inhabitants, with whom the Dyeths are interrelated) are tense in some places, and the north has been more sexually intolerant than the south (where the Dyeths live). In the north, gay and interspecies sex was recently illegal. On Rhyonon, gay male sex was illegal before age twenty-seven, but sex between tall and short people was particularly outlawed! (As it happens, Marq Dyeth is fairly short, and Rat Korga is very tall.[22] One aspect of their perfectly complementary predilections is their drastic difference from one another.) On Velm, interracial heterosexuality is the "most prominent perversion." Dyeth asks, "Will sex between humans ever lose its endlessly repeated history?" (211), a question that can be read back into many of Delany's earlier texts.

The quotation from Foucault cited in the previous section, having to do with the ascendancy of desire and the relative unimportance of acts, has its dangerous, demonic potentiality revealed very vividly for us in the character of Clym, one of "the odd creations of our epoch," as Dyeth calls him (98). Clym, with whom Dyeth has a sexual encounter involving some fairly elaborate perversions, is a professional, programmed psychotic assassin who makes few, if any, distinctions in the pursuit of his desire and no distinctions at all between work and pleasure. Clym finds Dyeth "strange" because his sexual preference is for a single gender of only a few species. Clym, on the other hand, finds the prospect of a world's entire population being destroyed "exciting" and warns Dyeth that, if they are still together, within the next few days he is going to torture him into mental and physical disfigurement, "though another woman, male or female, or any of several species of plants will replace you if you decide to leave" (96). The shock value of this sort of circumstance is to a great extent eroded by our realization early on that, in the words of the woman who buys Rat (illegally, since on Rhyonon only institutions can legally hold slaves), "anything's possible in this man's universe, right?" (23).[23]

The woman who buys Rat tells him that he can do anything he wants to sexually with her and that afterward she will do what she wants. This is nothing less than the licensing of unlimited desire (although in this instance, since Rat is gay, he has to "unlock" his desire by imagining that she is a man). However, it is in fact slavery itself which licenses desire by licensing mastery. It is not simply a matter of droit du seigneur, for the desire to maximize production by minimizing labor costs is definitely involved here—they are mastering men in order to master the environment—but it is a sexual matter also, for the rats are definitely exploited that way as well. One instance is the orgy that takes place the night before Rat, who has been "sold south" (a detail that gains a telling resonance from the history of Afro-American slavery), is due to leave. In a scene reminiscent of *Tides*, their boss employs Rat and his fellow rats in a debauch that involves having them whip the man and call him "a tiny rat" (16–17). One clear result of the degradation of the slave is the degradation of the master (as Reed satirically demonstrates in several of his novels).

After he is found, rescued, and healed by the Web, Rat announces, "You have given me the possibility of a world," and then asks, "What world will you give me?," warning that if he does not get one, he may take ten or more (172). What has given him the possibility of a world, as he puts it, is the set of rings formerly belonging to Vondramach Okk, the tyrant with whom Dyeth's principal ancestress, Mother Dyeth, was associated. The rings, designed to compensate for some of the severe damage Vondramach had done as a youth through the practice of self-mutilation, are able to compensate for the effects of Radical Anxiety Termination, hence dissolving Rat's formerly impoverished and restricted perspective.[24] He now has the possibility of grasping the world (whatever world he finds himself in), of knowing it, but it seems as if the rings also have imparted to him some of Vondramach's tyrannical personality, so that the idea of grasping a world, as it were, becomes literal in the sense of seizure, of conquest (Vondramach, after all, created an empire). I cannot help but relate Rat's statement to the black experience, for when the slaves were emancipated at the end of the Civil War, they were, in a powerful sense, given the possibility of a world in which they could function as persons, not objects. Reconstruction in the South was a brief, confused, and ultimately abortive effort to bring black people into the world that they had helped to create. The promise of the North was equally elusive. Although black people did indeed fashion a world for themselves out of their African inheritance and the syncretic genius that worked to transform whatever materials were at hand, it is the constantly unfulfilled promise of a world from which they have been, in varying degrees, excluded that has fueled the nationalistic and revolutionary impulses whose roots are antebellum. Possibilities offered but constantly unredeemed are challengingly potent.

The dragon hunt which Marq Dyeth takes Rat on is revealing yet again of the manner in which Delany's imaginative revisions lend new meaning to familiar concepts while at the same time illuminating crucial thematic concerns.

On Velm, dragons are related to evelmi, although they are not held to be intelligent. They have three sexes—male, female, neuter—any of which can bear offspring, and, unlike evelmi (but like the dragons in the Nevèrÿon stories), they can fly. Evelmi, disparagingly called "lizards" by human chauvinists like the Thant family, friends and rivals of the Dyeths, have six legs, claws, many tongues (which they can speak with simultaneously), and vestigial wings.

Human and evelmi cultures, we are told, are both founded on a love of illusion, and, indeed, one of the chief illusions is peace between their respective races, despite the fact (but presumably it is fairly exceptional) of a longstanding family bonding between humans and evelmi among the Dyeths. Humans and evelmi, in the recent past, hunted each other; both now hunt dragons, using radar-guided bows. Until the very moment when the quarry is in the sights and a "shot" is fired, the reader naturally assumes that this is a hunt in which there will be a kill, but Delany turns the tables on us beautifully, for, in fact, what the radar-bow does is track and map a dragon's cerebral responses, translate them, and play them back on the hunter's mind. You "catch" a dragon, then, by "becoming" one for few seconds, and the longer the joining, the more transcendental the experience. Afterward, in accordance with ancient evelmi practice, songs are sung about the experience which are improvised along traditional patterns. This ritual, celebrating the successful if momentary "embrace" of radical otherness, has great importance, for the urge to seek out (hunt) difference is not motivated here by a destructive impulse or a desire for a physical trophy, but rather by the challenge still involved in successfully tracking a dragon and the chance to lose oneself, even for an instant, in the turbulent poetry of an alien consciousness. (As Baraka has so aptly expressed it, "Hunting is not those heads on the wall.")

It is interesting that, shortly before they embark upon the hunt, Dyeth and Rat visit one of the "runs" where sex can be freely obtained, and while Dyeth (who has himself had sex with evelmi) watches, Rat has sex with an evelmi and another human male at the same time.[25] Interspecies sex, when the participants are all consenting adults of distinct, highly developed races, carries the question of miscegenation into a more complex dimension, although, from the perspective of people like the Thants, who come from a less progressive (or at least less behaviorally experimental) world, the Dyeths are degenerates who mate with "animals," who, in other words, commit bestiality; they are "lizard-lovers." It is easy to see that this is a future-worlds problem extrapolated from the present-day prejudice that interracial and homosexual relationships provoke. However, I think Delany is making another point here, in addition to demonstrating that sexual predilections are going to remain complex and the social attitudes toward them problematic; for, the intimacy between Dyeth and Rat notwithstanding (and it is well to remember that this is based in part on an extraordinary actuarial coincidence), sex is, in whatever permutations, a bodily act, while the sort of "coupling" that occurs during the successful drag hunt is a melding of consciousnesses, almost metaphysical in its implications. We can be intrigued by the other, we can love the other, but to see through the other's eyes is quite a different thing. Desire, like hatred, can—often must—precede understanding, if in fact the kind of understanding that creates equivalency is even possible.

Postscript

In a recent essay in *Critical Inquiry*, Ihab Hassan lists the following features of postmodernism: (1) indeterminacy, (2) fragmentation,

(3) decanonization (an assault on society's "mastercodes"), (4) self-lessness, depthlessness, (5) the unpresentable, unrepresentable, (6) irony, (7) hybridization, (8) carnivalization, (9) performance, participation, (10) constructionism ("worldmaking," the creation of fictions), and (11) immanence (semiotic replication) ("Pluralism in Postmodern Perspective," 504–508). Hassan is here refining ideas he originally offered in *Paracriticisms: Seven Speculations of the Times*, when he attempted to work out the emphases postmodernism has given to modernist concerns. One fact is at least clear in much current criticism: whatever postmodernism is—and despite certain contiguities, there is no complete agreement on a definition—it is, in any event, useful in forcing us to rethink what modernism was; so that we may perhaps have to await the advent of post-post-modernism before we can rightly comprehend postmodernism's difference. When Hassan informs us, then, that "criticism appears as much a discourse of desire as power" ("Pluralism," 511), one of the meanings has to do with criticism's own creative energies, its adoption of the allusiveness of the work of art, and its urge to work, so to say, ahead of itself to make clear that which is obscured by its own processes of becoming.

Fiction, even more so, has this quality of desire to reach beyond itself. LeRoi Jones/Amiri Baraka, Ishmael Reed, and Samuel R. Delany are all, to some degree, writers "in the thrall of the impossible real" (Blanchot, 38). However, language, which creates as it speaks, defies this "impossibility" and this "reality" equally, generating that radical alterity which is a significant portion of fiction's power.

Notes

Preliminaries

1. Compare André Brink, "Mapmakers." *Writing in a State of Siege: Essays on Politics and Literature.* New York: Summit, 1986.
2. Discussing a "rupture" experienced at the hands of academic critics who have an incomplete grasp of the genre's history, Delany argues that the assumption that SF "has no *significant* history" tends to reduce its difference from other phenomena ("Generic Protocols: Science Fiction and Mundane," 185). (This is similar to the arrogant Eurocentric assertion that

Africa had no history to speak of before the arrival of the white man, or that Afro-American history and other areas of Black Studies have no proper basis of their own.) One of the aspects of SF that is particularly significant, Delany further argues, is that it exhibits a plurality of styles and strives for a plurality of values ("Protocols," 188).

3. Referring to "the eternal dialectic," Ihab Hassan asks, "But why not a trialectic, for instance, or multilectic?" (*Paracriticism*, xi–xii). In Delany's work, there is a vision not only of multiplexity (the last term in the conceptual triad of simplex–complex–multiplex) but also of "trialogue" (*Neveryóna*, 290), which I think has to be read both as tri/alogue (a triangular relationship—triads always have been symbolically important for Delany) and trial/ogue (a struggle, a determination).

4. Ihab Hassan cites Buckminster Fuller's claim that man is faced with a choice between utopia and oblivion (*Paracriticisms*, 110). Utopia indeed may be unattainable, but it is the necessary direction in which we must move, as Delany demonstrates in his radical visions of societal transformation. The alternative (which Delany calls "cultural fugue") means the literal death of a world. Given the means of total annihilation, man must either transcend himself or face the unthinkable consequences of his self-destructive tendencies.

5. For a more detailed analysis of *Dhalgren* and the novels which preceded it, see "The Mirrors of Caliban" (in Works Cited).

The Tides of Lust

6. "Literature of the fantastic is concerned to describe desire in its excessive forms as well as its various transformations or . . . perversions" (Todorov, 138).

7. There is a Joaquim Faust in *Dhalgren* who describes himself as "A grandpa Yippie, yeah? I'm a traveling philosopher" (80).

8. For further remarks on this novel, see my essay "The Politics of Desire in Delany's *Triton* and *The Tides of Lust*," *Black American Literature Forum* 18, no. 2 (1984): 49–56.

Tales of the Modular Calculus

9. "Vlet" may be an anagram of "velt," a word of German origin meaning "field," from whence "veldt," the Afrikaans word for the South African grasslands. The German word for "world" is "Welt." The world-field of action is doubled by the word-field of language, each embodying play.

One suspects that game theory is operating here: combinations, permutations, complex models. The strategies are linguistic; the stakes, aesthetic and liberational. The risks Delany takes with ideas, the free rein he allows his imagination, the precise focus he affords us through what Césaire calls "the eye of words," are the sorts of striving also demanded of his characters by the realms of freedom and restraint they inhabit, which, in various ways, mirror our own turbulent times.

10. With reference to the slave collar, it is interesting to note that the Norse word for "free" is derived from another term meaning "free-neck" (Patterson, 216).

The slave collar is round, suggesting the endlessness of desire, the way in which it seeks as fully as possible to surround (enclose) its subject as well as its object.

11. If it is true, as psychologists today generally believe, that the first few months of life are crucial in determining the fate of an adult personality, might it not also be the case that the fate of mankind's character was determined in the early years of human existence? *Homo faber* keeps transcending himself, but as a social being, man remains persistently problematic.

12. Gorgik was a slave in the Child Empress's obsidian mines: digging black stone, freeing its "value." This detail is suggestive of the way in which black artists have slaved away for years, often neglected and despised, yet still mining blackness for all its possibilities, its limning and liberating potential.

13. Delany is very good at exposing the reactionary nature of many of our attitudes and institutions by counterpointing them with more libertarian forms of behavior in his suppositional futures. One of his points is that although we think that we are on the cutting edge of experience because we are in the now, unless we are able to really break through the entrapments of our conditioned patterns of belief, whether acquiescent or dissident, the future will see us as merely another backward world of transcendental flights of fancy but transformative failures.

14. For a more detailed analysis of *Triton*, see my essay "The Politics of Desire," cited above.

15. Delany's Culhar' fragment, supposed to predate Homer and Gilgamesh, corresponds to Foucault's concept of an original or primal Text which underlies and provides the basis for the "commentary" of writing (*The Order of Things: An Archaeology of the Human Sciences*, 41).

16. To unfold, to explicate: from *explicare*. Explication and speculation are a dual process here, both in Delany's work and my examination of it.

In appendix B to *Flight from Nevèrÿon*, Delany explains the structure of the trilogy as follows: the stories in *Tales of Nevèrÿon* constitute a study of the way in which signs are organized; *Nevèrÿona* is a study of the way in which signs are generated; and *Flight* deals with "the excess, the leftover, the supplement of linguistics" (357–358). He also makes explicit the fact that the whole series is a model of our current American reality, a model which he terms "Rich, eristic, and contestatory (as *well* as documentary)" (377).

17. In Jones's fiction, women play only marginal or peripheral roles; the turbulence of male ego is always central. In Reed's novels, when women are prominent, they are, for the most part, problems—adversaries of takin'-care-of-Business men. Delany alone is comfortable putting women in strong, affirmative roles in his writings, sometimes at the expense of certain male characters who suffer by comparison. (In *Triton*, for example, Bron Helstrom is clearly not the "equal" of Gene Trimbell, the Spike.) It is difficult not to connect these attitudes with the authors' own sexual predilections. Although Jones was able to employ homosexuality in nonpejorative ways in his early work, his metamorphosis into Amiri Baraka and his emphatic embrace of black consciousness entailed a rejection of homosexuality. Delany, on the contrary, has become more unequivocally gay as he actively engaged liberational strategies in life and language. Reed remains outside of this dichotomy, in steadfastly heterosexual territory.

18. Reed's Raven Quickskill is so named partly to connect him with the raven creator of Tlingit myth; the raven is Quickskill's totem. Since Delany's Raven is the one who narrates her people's genesis story, it is hard not to make a connection here, too, with the raven (a black god) as a symbol of creative power.

19. Sword-and-sorcery here yields to pen-and-sorcery (the violence of the letter, writing as magic), and Delany's use of a word-processor as a compositional tool only intensifies the magico-technological thrust of civilization's wave-form. Furthermore, the potentially phallogocentric bias underlying the equation sword≈penis≈pen is elided by Delany through the vaginal symbolism of Raven's double-bladed weapon and the deep involvement of women in the invention of writing.

Stars in My Pocket Like Grains of Sand

20. Spiders are arachnids. (In Greek mythology, Arachne was a woman so skilled in weaving that she rivaled the goddess Athena, who destroyed her web. Arachne thereupon hanged herself, and Athena transformed her into a spider.) However, there is a delicate, weblike membrane of the spinal cord and brain called the arachnoid. The Web, then, is a kind of cosmic mind membrane, created (spun) by "spiders."

21. Radical Anxiety Termination reminded me of the practice of lobotomy, an operation employed for much the same reason—to render the troublesome tranquil. By an interesting coincidence, shortly after the pub-

lication of *Stars in My Pocket*, a book appeared that documents the "career" of psychosurgery, another instance of the fact that speculative fiction remains on the firing line of social issues in its extrapolation of problematic aspects of human experience. (See *Great and Desperate Cures: The Rise and Decline of Psychosurgery and Other Radical Treatments for Mental Illness* by Elliot S. Valenstein.)

22. Dyeth is described as short and stocky, with blonde, nappy hair and tan eyes (80). We also are informed that about one-fifth of the human race was once caucasian, but from the manner in which this information is imparted, one is led to assume that such "pale skins" are now rare (80). It is typical of Delany to employ such subtle means to convey racial details. It suggests that genetics and demographics are going to do more to resolve the race problem than politics.

23. Her use of "man" is, it must be recalled, a sign of the social and linguistic backwardness of her world. However, Delany clearly shows us that anything is possible in the wider universe of "women" as well.

24. The self-mutilation practiced by Vondramach Okk brings to mind the self-mutilation of Ashima Slade in *Triton*. One wonders about this kind of fascination in Delany's work. Given medical advancements in which people can make frequent replacements of parts of themselves if necessary, would such self-abusive practices become common as "art," as "self-expression"? In fact, "body art," as one category of performance art, is already involving elements of personal danger and possible personal damage; consider, for example, the work of Chris Burden, who has had himself crucified on a car, has crawled naked through broken glass, and pushed two live wires into his chest, to name a few acts he has done.

25. Sex in the "runs" is free, but Bron Helstrom was a practicing male prostitute, and prostitutes of both sexes ply their trade on the Bridge of Lost Desire in the Nevèrÿon stories. In *Flight from Nevèrÿon*, prostitutes are referred to as "sexual workers," and the business of sex (both implying and transcending economics) is called sexual "commerce" (140–141), a more revealing term than "intercourse"; it reminds us of the suggestion that "commerce, lust, madness, travel" are the essential topics of urban life (153). The Marxistic usage, "sexual worker," does not define prostitution as a form of oppression but rather legitimizes it, for it is clear from many of Delany's writings that whatever the economic system, whatever the era, whatever the world, the professional as well as free exchange of sex is a fact of life that needs to be accepted.

Works Cited

Abrahams, Roger D. *The Man-of-Words in the West Indies: Performance and the Emergence of Creole Culture*. Baltimore: Johns Hopkins University Press, 1983.

Adelugba, Dapo. "Trance and Theatre: The Nigerian Experience." In *Drama and Theatre in Nigeria*, edited by Yemi Ogunbiyi. Lagos: Nigeria Magazine, 1981. 203–218.

Anozie, Sunday O. *Structural Models and African Poetics*. London: Routledge & Kegan Paul, 1981.

Armah, Ayi Kwei. *Two Thousand Seasons*. Nairobi: East Africa Publishing House, 1973; rpt. Chicago: Third World, 1979.

Baker, Houston A., Jr. *The Journey Back: Issues in Black Literature and Criticism*. Chicago: University of Chicago Press, 1980.

Baraka, Amiri. *The Autobiography of LeRoi Jones/Amiri Baraka*. New York: Freundlich, 1984.

———. "Blank." *Callaloo* 8, no. 2 (1985): 281–293.

———. *Daggers and Javelins: Essays, 1974–1979*. New York: Quill, 1984.

———. *Kawaida Studies: The New Nationalism*. Chicago: Third World, 1972.

———. *Raise Race Rays Raze: Essays Since 1965*. New York: Random House, 1971.

———. *Selected Poetry of Amiri Baraka/LeRoi Jones*. New York: Morrow, 1979.

———, and Amina Baraka. *Confirmation: An Anthology of African American Women*. New York: Quill, 1983.

Barthes, Roland. *A Lover's Discourse: Fragments*. Translated by Richard Howard. New York: Hill & Wang, 1984.

Baudrillard, Jean. "The Precession of Simulacra." In *Art After Modernism: Rethinking Representation*, edited by Brian Wallis. New York: The New Museum of Contemporary Art, 1984, 253–281.

Blanchot, Maurice. *The Writing of the Disaster.* Translated by Ann Smock. Lincoln: University of Nebraska Press, 1986.

Brain, Robert. *Art and Society in Africa.* New York: Longman, 1980.

Bray, Mary Kay. "Rites of Reversal: Double Consciousness in Delany's *Dhalgren.*" *Black American Literature Forum* 18, no. 2 (1984): 57–61.

Brown, William Wells. *Clotel; or, The President's Daughter: A Narrative of Slave Life in the United States.* New York: Macmillan, 1970.

Byerman, Keith E. *Fingering the Jagged Edge: Tradition and Form in Recent Black Fiction.* Athens: The University of Georgia Press, 1985.

Cade, Toni. "The Pill: Genocide or Liberation." In *The Black Woman,* edited by Toni Cade. New York: New American Liberary, 1970. 162–169.

Cartey, Wilfred. *Black Images.* New York: Teachers College Press, 1970.

Castle, Terry. "The Carnivalization of Eighteenth-Century Narrative." *PMLA* 99, no. 5 (1984): 903–916.

Cavell, Stanley. "The Fantastic of Philosophy." *The American Poetry Review* 15, no. 3 (1986): 45–47.

Childs, John Brown. "Afro-American Intellectuals and the People's Culture." *Theory and Society* 13, no. 1 (1984): 69–90.

Clarke, Cheryl. "The Failure to Transform: Homophobia in the Black Community." In *Home Girls: A Black Feminist Anthology,* edited by Barbara Smith. New York: Kitchen Table, 1983. 197–208.

Creeley, Robert. *The Collected Prose of Robert Creeley.* New York: Marion Boyars, 1984.

Davis, David Brion. *The Problem of Slavery in the Age of Revolution, 1770–1823.* Ithaca, N.Y.: Cornell University Press, 1975.

Delany, Samuel R. *Babel-17.* New York: Ace, 1966.

———. *Dhalgren.* New York: Bantam, 1975.

———. *Empire Star,* New York: Ace, 1966.

———. *Flight from Nevèryon.* New York: Bantam, 1985.

———. "Generic Protocols: Science Fiction and Mundane." In *The Technological Imagination: Theories and Fictions,* edited by Teresa de Lauretis, Andreas Huyssen, and Kathleen Woodward. Madison: Coda Press, 1980. 175–193.

———. *Neveryóna.* New York: Bantam, 1983.

———. *Nova.* Garden City, N.Y.: Doubleday, 1968.

———. *Stars in My Pocket Like Grains of Sand.* New York: Bantam, 1984.

———. *Tales of Nevèryon.* New York: Bantam, 1979.

———. *The Tides of Lust.* Manchester: Savoy, 1980.

———. *Triton.* New York: Bantam, 1976.

Douglas, Ann. "The Art of Controversy." Introduction to *Uncle Tom's Cabin or, Life Among the Lowly,* Harriet Beecher Stowe. New York: Penguin American Library, 1981.

Dreyfus, Hubert L., and Paul Rabinow. *Michel Foucault: Beyond Structuralism and Hermeneutics.* 2d ed. Chicago: University of Chicago Press, 1983.

Eagleton, Terry. *Criticism and Ideology.* London: Verso, 1978.

Ellison, Ralph. *Invisible Man.* New York: Modern Library, 1952.

Fish, Stanley. *Surprised by Sin: The Reader in Paradise Lost.* London: Macmillan, 1967.

Foster, Hal. *Recodings: Art, Spectacle, Cultural Politics.* Port Townsend, Washington: Bay Press, 1985.

Foucault, Michel. *The Order of Things: An Archeaology of the Human Sciences.* New York: Vintage, 1973.

Fox, Robert Elliot. "The Mirrors of Caliban: A Study of the Fiction of LeRoi Jones (Imamu Amiri Baraka), Ishmael Reed, and Samuel R. Delany." Ph.D. dissertation, State University of New York at Buffalo, 1976.

Gablik, Suzi. *Has Modernism Failed?* New York: Thames and Hudson, 1984.

Garon, Paul. *Blues and the Poetic Spirit.* New York: Da Capo, 1979.

Gass, William H. "The Face of the City." *Harper's,* March 1986: 37–39, 42–46.

Gates, Henry Louis, Jr. "The 'Blackness of Blackness': A Critique of the Sign and the Signifying Monkey." *Critical Inquiry* 9, no. 4 (1983): 685–723.

Girard, Rene., *Deceit, Desire, and the Novel: Self and Other in Literary Structure.* Translated by Yvonne Freccero. Baltimore: Johns Hopkins University Press, 1965.

Goss, Clay. *Mars. Kuntu Drama: Plays of the African Continuum.* Edited by Paul Carter Harrison. New York: Grove Press, 1974. 241–255.

Graff, Gerald. *Literature Against Itself: Literary Ideas in Modern Society.* Chicago: University of Chicago Press, 1981.

Gwaltney, John Langston. *Drylongso: A Self-Portrait of Black America.* New York: Random House, 1980.

Harris, Wilson. *The Tree of the Sun.* London: Faber and Faber, 1978.

Harrison, Paul. *Inside the Third World.* 2d ed. New York: Penguin, 1981.

Hartman, Geoffrey H. *Saving the Text: Literature/Derrida/Philosophy.* Baltimore: Johns Hopkins University Press, 1981.

Hartsock, Nancy C. M. *Money, Sex, and Power: Toward a Feminist Historical Materialism.* Boston: Northeastern University Press, 1985.

Hassan, Ihab. *Paracriticisms: Seven Speculations of the Times.* Urbana: University of Illinois Press, 1975.

———. "Pluralism in Postmodern Perspective." *Critical Inquiry* 12, no. 3 (1986): 503–520.

Hayden, Robert. *Collected Poems.* Edited by Frederick Glaysher. New York: Liveright, 1985.

Henry, Jules. *Culture Against Man*. New York: Vintage, 1965.

Hernton, Calvin. "The Sexual Mountain and Black Women Writers." *The Black Scholar* 16, no. 4 (1985): 2–11.

Hoberman, J. "After Avant-Garde Film." In *Art After Modernism*, edited by Brian Wallis. New York: The New Museum of Contemporary Art, 1984. 59–73.

Horn, Andrew, "Ritual, Drama, and the Theatrical: The Case of *Bori* Spirit Mediumship." In *Drama and Theatre in Nigeria*, edited by Yemi Ogunbiyi. Lagos: Nigeria Magazine, 1981. 181–202.

Hubbard, Dolan. "An Interview with Richard K. Barksdale." *Black American Literature Forum* 19, no. 4 (1985): 139–145.

Hudson, Theodore R. *From LeRoi Jones to Amiri Baraka: The Literary Works*. Durham, N.C.: Duke University Press, 1973.

Jahn, Janheinz. "Residual African Elements in the Blues." In *Mother Wit from the Laughing Barrel: Readings in the Interpretation of Afro-American Folklore*, edited by Alan Dundes. New York: Garland, 1981. 97–103.

Jameson, Fredric. "Postmodernism and Consumer Society." In *The Anti-Aesthetic: Essays on Postmodern Culture*, edited by Hal Foster. Port Townsend, Washington: Bay Press, 1983. 111–125.

Jones, Ann Rosalind. "Writing the Body: Toward an Understanding of *l'Ecriture feminine*." In *The New Feminist Criticism: Essays on Women, Literature, and Theory*, edited by Elaine Showalter. New York: Pantheon, 1985. 361–377.

Jones, LeRoi. *The Moderns: An Anthology of New Writing in America*. New York: Corinth, 1963.

———. *The System of Dante's Hell*. New York: Grove Press, 1965.

———. *Tales*. New York: Grove Press, 1967.

Jussim, Estelle. "The Self-Reflexive Camera." *Boston Review* 11, no. 2 (1986): 12–14, 26.

Keil, Charles. *Urban Blues*. Chicago: University of Chicago Press, 1966.

Kristeva, Julia. "Women's Time." Translated by Alice Jardine and Harry Blake. In *Feminist Theory: A Critique of Ideology*, edited by Nannerl O. Keohane, Michelle Z. Rosaldo, and Barbara Gelpi. Chicago: University of Chicago Press, 1982. 31–53.

Lacey, Henry C. *To Raise, Destroy, and Create: The Poetry, Drama, and Fiction of Imamu Amiri Baraka (LeRoi Jones)*. Troy, N.Y.: Whitston, 1981.

Lamy, Lucie. *Egyptian Mysteries*. New York: Crossroad, 1981.

Leitch, Vincent B. *Deconstructive Criticism: An Advanced Introduction*. New York: Columbia University Press, 1983.

McClusky, Pamela. *Praise Poems: The Katherine White Collection*. Seattle: Seattle Art Museum, 1984.

McKay, Claude. *Gingertown*. New York: Harper & Bros., 1932; rpt. Freeport, N.Y.: Books for Libraries Press, 1972.

———. *A Long Way from Home*. New York: Lee Furman, 1937; rpt. New York: Arno, 1969.

Miller, Christopher L. *Blank Darkness: Africanist Discourse in French*. Chicago: University of Chicago Press, 1985.

Mitchell, Donald. *The Language of Modern Music*. London: Faber, 1976.

Murray, Albert. *Stomping the Blues*. New York: Vintage, 1982.

Nazareth, Peter. "Heading Them Off at the Pass: The Fiction of Ishmael Reed." *The Review of Contemporary Fiction* 4, no. 2 (1984): 208–226.

Newman, Charles. *The Post-Modern Aura: The Act of Fiction in an Age of Inflation*. Evanston: Northwestern University Press, 1985.

O'Keefe, Daniel Lawrence. *Stolen Lightning: The Social Theory of Magic*. New York: Vintage, 1983.

Olney, James. " 'I Was Born': Slave Narratives, Their Status as Autobiography and as Literature." *Callaloo* 7, no. 1 (1984): 46–73.

Ornstein, Robert E. *The Psychology of Consciousness*. Harmondsworth: Penguin, 1975.

Patterson, Orlando. *Slavery and Social Death: A Comparative Study*. Cambridge: Harvard University Press, 1982.

Reed, Ishmael. "Cab Calloway Stands In for the Moon." In *19 Necromancers from Now*, edited by Ishmael Reed. Garden City, N.Y.: Doubleday, 1970. 293–309.

———. *Chattanooga*. New York: Random House, 1973.

———. *Conjure*. Amherst: University of Massachusetts Press, 1972.

———. "Flight to Canada." In *American Poets in 1976*, edited by William Heyen. Indianapolis: Bobbs-Merrill, 1976. 264–274.

———. *Flight to Canada*. New York: Random House, 1976.

———. *The Freelance Pallbearers*. Garden City, N.Y.: Doubleday, 1967.

———. *God Made Alaska for the Indians: Selected Essays*. New York: Garland, 1982.

———. *The Last Days of Louisiana Red*. New York: Random House, 1974.

———. *Mumbo Jumbo*, Garden City, N.Y.: Doubleday, 1972.

———. *Reckless Eyeballing*. New York: St. Martin's, 1986.

———. *Shrovetide in Old New Orleans*. Garden City, N.Y.: Doubleday, 1978.

———. *The Terrible Twos*. New York: St. Martin's/Marek, 1982.

Rigaud, Milo. *Secrets of Voodoo*. San Francisco: City Lights, 1985.

Russ, Joanna. *How to Suppress Women's Writing*. Austin: University of Texas Press, 1983.

Shange, Ntozake. *Sassafrass, Cypress, and Indigo*. New York: St. Martin's, 1982.

Shattuck, Roger. *The Innocent Eye: On Modern Literature and the Arts.* New York: Washington Square, 1986.

Sollors, Werner. *Amiri Baraka/LeRoi Jones: The Quest for a "Populist Modernism."* New York: Columbia University Press, 1978.

Steiner, George. *Antigone.* New York: Oxford, 1984.

Tate, Claudia. "Toni Cade Bambara." *Black Women Writers at Work.* New York: Continuum, 1983. 12–38.

Teish, Luisa. *Jambalaya: The Natural Woman's Book of Personal Charms and Practical Rituals.* San Francisco: Harper & Row, 1985.

Thompson, Robert Farris. *African Art in Motion: Icon and Act.* Berkeley: University of California Press, 1974.

Thompson, William Irwin. *Passages about Earth: An Exploration of the New Planetary Culture.* New York: Harper & Row, 1981.

————. *The Time Falling Bodies Take to Light: Mythology, Sexuality, and the Origins of Culture.* New York: St. Martin's, 1981.

Todorov, Tzvetan. *The Fantastic: A Structural Approach to a Literary Genre.* Translated by Richard Howard. Cleveland: Case Western Reserve University Press, 1973.

Toll, Robert C. *Blacking Up: The Minstrel Show in Nineteenth-Century America.* New York: Oxford, 1974.

Turner, Victor. *From Ritual to Theatre: The Human Seriousness of Play.* New York: Performing Arts Journal Publications, 1982.

Ulmer, Gregory L. *Applied Grammatology: Post(e)-Pedagogy from Jacques Derrida to Joseph Beuys.* Baltimore: Johns Hopkins University Press, 1985.

Webb, Frank J. *The Garies and Their Friends,* London: Routledge, 1857; rpt. New York: Arno, 1969.

Zamyatin, Yevgeny. *A Soviet Heretic: Essays by Yevgeny Zamyatin.* Edited and translated by Mirra Ginsburg. Chicago: University of Chicago Press, 1970.

Index

Not Without Laughter (Hughes), 2,
   59
Novalis, 110

Ogun (Yoruba deity), 62
O'Hara, Frank, 17
Olney, James, 50–51, 72
Olson, Charles, 17, 18
Order of Things, The (Foucault),
   123
Osiris, 51, 54, 61

Paracriticisms (Hassan), 121, 122
Paradise Lost (Milton), 12
Parker, Charlie (Yardbird), 51–52
Parker, Junior, 88
Passages About Earth (W. I.
   Thompson), 94
Patterson, Orlando, 106
Picasso, Pablo, 88
Plato, 54, 100
Pl/atonism, 26, 56
Poe, Edgar Allan, 68, 95
Pop Art, 83, 93
Pornography and Silence (Griffin),
   100
Postmodernism, 8–9, 93, 97, 103,
   114
   characterized, 120–121
   in New Wave SF, 99–100
   and pluralism, 9
Pound, Ezra, 11
Prynne, Hester, 113

Rainey, Ma, 66
Rastafarianism, 77
Read, Herbert, 30
Reagan, Ronald, 75, 76, 78, 80
Reed, Ishmael, 1, 2, 3, 4, 5, 7, 8,
   11, 12, 15, 20, 25, 26, 32, 35,
   36, 39, 40, 43, 68, 71, 75, 77,
   78, 81, 82, 88, 90, 91, 95, 96,

99, 104, 107, 108, 110, 118,
   121, 123
   criticism of capitalism, 76
   declining powers, 79
   fictional strategy, 44, 83
   importance of, 87
   influence of black music on, 16
   influence of media on, 83, 93
   as misogynist, 84–87
   multicultural perspective, 6, 41
   novels, improvisational charac-
      ter of, 48
   opposed to cultural chauvinism,
      30–31
   position on women, 62–66
   and postmodernism, 9
Reed, Ishmael, works
   The Ace Boons, 91
   "Cab Calloway Stands In For
      the Moon," 51; Noxon, 59;
      Rin Tin Rover, 51
   Chattanooga, 71
   "Flight to Canada," 71; Porke
      plantation, 71; John Swell, 71
   Flight to Canada, 3, 20, 68–75,
      87, 97, 99, 107; as parody of
      slave narrative, 51, 68, 87
   The Freelance Pallbearers, 3, 25,
      39–44, 57, 59, 62, 68, 75; ex-
      cremental vision of, 42; The
      Freelance Pallbearers, 44; Na-
      zarene apocalypse, 41; Naza-
      rene Creed, 39, 40–41, 73; as
      parody of *Invisible Man*, 36,
      40–41; as parody of *Up From
      Slavery*, 39
   God Made Alaska For the Indians,
      90
   Hell Hath No Fury, 91
   The Last Days of Louisiana Red,
      20, 52, 59–68, 72, 73; antima-
      triarchal bias, 62–66; based on
      Antigone, 60–61, 62–64, 65;

About the Author

ROBERT ELLIOT FOX is an Assistant Professor of English at Suffolk University in Boston, where he also serves as Director of the Collection of Afro-American Literature. From 1978 to 1985 he taught at the University of Ife in Nigeria, where he was Senior Lecturer and Director of Graduate Studies.